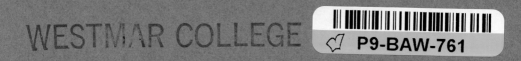

For Henry Veatch

Was du ererbt von deinen Vätern hast,
Erwirb es, um es zu besitzen!

Faust, 682 f.

Kant, Ontology, & the A Priori

MOLTKE S. GRAM

Northwestern University Press

EVANSTON · MCMLXVIII

COPYRIGHT © 1968 BY MOLTKE S. GRAM
ALL RIGHTS RESERVED
LIBRARY OF CONGRESS CATALOG CARD NUMBER 68–29324
MANUFACTURED IN THE UNITED STATES OF AMERICA

*Moltke S. Gram is Assistant Professor of Philosophy
at Northwestern University, Evanston, Illinois*

CONTENTS

PREFACE

THIS BOOK has grown out of a dissatisfaction with the concentration on Kant's theory of dialectic as the source of paradigm cases of metaphysical propositions. This has made it possible to look upon the *Kritik* as offering on the one hand a theory of the propositions which are the basis of natural science and mathematics and on the other hand a theory of propositions which metaphysicians had falsely thought to be verifiable. And the result of this division is to obscure what I believe to be Kant's own theory of metaphysical propositions as distinct from the propositions which may form the presuppositions of a special science or the propositions which are metaphysical in character but unverifiable. Kant tells us that metaphysical propositions are about an object in general. But the propositions which Kant examines in the Transcendental Dialectic are about particular objects: the soul, the totality of appearances, and God. And the propositions which form the basis of particular sciences are not about an object in general but rather about particular kinds of objects. Neither of these kinds of propositions can illustrate the results of the program of reform in metaphysics which Kant intended to initiate by writing the *Kritik*. The task I have set myself in this book is to show in what sense Kant is offering a theory of metaphysical propositions about objects in general.

There are primarily two tendencies in the philosophical scholarship on the *Kritik* against which the present book is a reaction. There is, first of all, a line of interpretation begun by Alois Riehl in his *Der philosophische Kritizismus: Geschichte und System.*[1] Riehl argued that the *Kritik* shows that metaphysics can never be a discipline since its concepts have no application to experience. This interpretation of the theory of metaphysics to be found in the *Kritik* found what was perhaps its most famous exposition in Hermann Cohen's *Kants Theorie der Erfahrung.*[2] Cohen saw the *Kritik* as an attempt to arrive at the presuppositions of scientific and mathematical knowledge. The step from Riehl to Cohen was a natural one: Once you have been convinced that Kant showed the impossibility of proof in metaphysics, then the only recourse you can have with the propositions which Kant did think possible of proof is to call them presuppositions of scientific and mathematical knowledge.

What has always troubled me about this way of interpreting Kant's theory of metaphysical propositions is that it does justice neither to Kant's theory of metaphysics nor to his theory of the presuppositions of extrametaphysical knowledge. The picture we are given by Cohen cannot explain, for example, why the propositions which Kant believes to constitute the presuppositions of extrametaphysical knowledge in fact contain such concepts as those of cause and substance—both of which traditionally belong to the domain of metaphysics. To say,

1. Alois Riehl, *Der philosophische Kritizismus: Geschichte und System* (3d ed.; Leipzig: A Kroner, 1924–26).
2. Hermann Cohen, *Kants Theorie der Erfahrung* (4th ed.; Berlin: B. Cassirer, 1925).

then, that Kant rejects the possibility of proof in metaphysics would force us to say that he implicitly rejects the propositions he proves in the Transcendental Analytic as metaphysical even though they contain concepts which he would call metaphysical. But this is not the only difficulty with the line of interpretation under consideration: It also distorts Kant's notion of what counts as a presupposition of extra-metaphysical knowledge. If the presuppositions which he seeks to prove in the Transcendental Analytic are not metaphysical, then we cannot explain how Kant could have thought, as he did think, that the concepts constituting the categories were metaphysical.

What I have just described is not, however, the only tendency in Kant scholarship which has caused my dissatisfaction with the received accounts of Kant's theory of metaphysics. Others before me have tried to shed light on Kant's theory of metaphysics; but what has emerged as the most famous attempt to do this, Martin Heidegger's *Kant und das Problem der Metaphysik*,[3] omits what I consider to be the most characteristic features of Kant's theory. Heidegger argues that the *Kritik* gives us an ontology understood as an account of man's place in the world. And when Kant shows that certain classes of propositions are in principle unverifiable because of the limitations placed upon our cognition, Heidegger takes this to show the finitude of man's place in the world. Thus the kind of metaphysical theory which the *Kritik* propounds is an elaboration of man's finite cognitive capacities to grasp Being.

My difficulty with Heidegger is not that what he says is false but rather that it is radically incomplete as an account of Kant's doctrine of metaphysical propositions. Kant does, indeed, argue that we must restrict the range of application of metaphysical propositions if we are to show whether they are true or false. And this does remind us of our finitude; but it does not show us how such a restriction works in practice as a way of demonstrating propositions which are about the world and not about man's place in the world. And although such propositions may, as Heidegger insists, imply something about man's

3. Martin Heidegger, *Kant und das Problem der Metaphysik* (Bonn: F. Cohen, 1929).

place in the world, they do so only by first telling us what is in the world and the extent of our knowledge of it.

My indebtedness to previous writers on Kant is great, although I have occasion to criticize much of what they have said. The work of Lewis White Beck was, in both its precision and its philosophical relevance, decisive in first turning my interest to Kant and throughout my study of Kant has served as a standard of excellence which has been only imperfectly realized in the present work. My debt to his work is very great.

I am also indebted to Professor Newton P. Stallknecht, under whose direction several of the chapters of this book took shape as part of a doctoral dissertation. And I should also like to acknowledge here how much the philosophical acuity of my former teacher, Alan Donagan, has meant to me, both during the time I spent studying with him and later, when his criticism and philosophical guidance helped me in writing this book. What he has given to me has made this a very much better book than it would otherwise have been. And my editor, Mrs. Virginia Seidman of Northwestern University Press, has saved me from more pitfalls than I want to acknowledge. I am, alas, solely responsible for whatever errors remain.

The quotations from Kant in the book have the following sources. All quotations from the first *Kritik* are taken from the Norman Kemp Smith translation. Quotations from other parts of the Kantian corpus are my translations from the Cassirer edition of Kant's works. References to the *Nachlass* are to the numbering which the items have in *Kant's Gesammelte Schriften*, edited by the Prussian Academy of Sciences.

M. S. Gram

Evanston, Illinois
February 1968

Kant, Ontology, and the *A Priori*

CHAPTER ONE

Introduction

WE HAVE OFTEN BEEN REMINDED that the *Kritik der reinen Vernunft* effected a revolution in metaphysical method. Kant himself frequently enough tells us this, saying, for example, that "this attempt to alter the procedure which has hitherto prevailed in metaphysics . . . forms the main purpose of this critique."[1] The character of this revolution has been traced over often enough to have assumed an easily recognizable and standard form. It goes, roughly, like this. Kant's problem about metaphysics was that it contained propositions whose truth or falsity could not be shown either by inspecting the terms or concepts composing them or

---

1. Bxxii; cf. *Prolegomena*, Appendix, in *Immanuel Kants Werke*, edited by Ernst Cassirer (11 vols.; Berlin: Cassirer Verlag, 1921–22), IV, 128 ff. (cited hereafter as "*Werke*").

by an appeal to what is in the world. For propositions which can be falsified or verified by analyzing the terms composing them tell us nothing about the way the world is; and propositions which can be verified only by an appeal to the way the world is can tell us only about what is true of particular matters of fact, not about what is true of every matter of fact. And so traditional metaphysics was distinguished by a kind of proposition which purported to tell us what is universally and necessarily true of the world; yet, at the same time, traditional metaphysics did not tell us how we could ever know that such a proposition was true or false.

The revolution that Kant brought about was to show the verification of which these typically metaphysical claims admitted. Thus although nothing in experience corresponds to the concepts contained in typically metaphysical propositions, they can none the less be shown to be true or false once it is shown that they state the necessary conditions under which experience of any particular object is possible. And this is what distinguishes a metaphysical proposition from any other kind of proposition about the world. While the latter tells us something about the world, it does not state a necessary condition of our experience of the world.

The account I have just traced is, as it stands, not inaccurate. But this account usually contains more definite theses about the character of Kant's doctrine, which I shall summarize as follows:

1. A metaphysical proposition is synthetic in that the two concepts composing it are not analytically related to each other.
2. The concepts composing a metaphysical proposition are pure categories; they are thus not concepts of determinate objects in intuition but are rather concepts of an object in general.
3. Synthetic propositions which are composed of pure categories must relate to a fact by which the combination of such concepts in the proposition can be justified. But since pure categories refer only to an object in general, there can be no fact in experience by reference to which we can justify their combination in the proposition.

4. Metaphysical propositions are verified only by reference to the possibility of experience.

The account which I just summarized has become standard for the understandable reason that it is supported by many things that Kant himself says. But one of the principal claims that I shall defend in what follows is that such an account, if it is thought through, makes it unintelligible why Kant himself or, for that matter, anyone else should have thought that Kant succeeded in offering a genuine reform in metaphysical method. Thus I shall argue that, if we are to understand the character and import of Kant's program in metaphysics, it is essential to see that what I have called the standard account of that program fits the text, if at all, then only very loosely. For one thing, the standard account is not able to explain why Kant, in many of the major passages of the *Kritik*, argued as he did. For another, the account is not able to explain how the position Kant defends in the *Kritik* can ultimately be distinguished from the very kind of method in metaphysics to which it was to be an alternative. Both of these reasons are, I believe, enough to discredit the usual account of Kant's reform in metaphysics.

But the standard account which I wish to reject is not, I must add, merely a *Hirngespinst* of the commentators. It is, in large part, an account sanctioned by Kant himself. Once the character of this sanction is understood, however, it will not be enough to support the standard account. When I say that the account in question is sanctioned by Kant himself, what I mean is that the account is drawn from what Kant *says* that he is doing rather than what he in fact does. What the account overlooks is the crucial disparity between the way in which Kant seeks to formulate his program of metaphysical reform and the way in which he argues for that program. The result of overlooking this is, as I shall argue, to give an account of Kant's program that obscures its actual character and hence blinds us to its philosophical significance. The plan of the present book, then, is this. I shall take up each of the parts of the standard account in turn, ask what justification it has in Kant's text, and show how it diverges, if not from Kant's own description, then from the procedure he follows. My main exegetical task will be to construct an account that will more faithfully reflect the character of Kant's program and explain why Kant could have misdescribed what he was doing in several of the main arguments by which he tries to establish that program.

But what exactly are the defects which vitiate the received account of Kant's reform in metaphysics? The first deficiency is found in the account given of Kant's analysis of judgment. Here Kant supports the usual account: All judgments are composed of concepts which are related to each other by inclusion or exclusion. This is, indeed, how Kant characterizes the distinction between synthetic and analytic judgments. But this characterization is not compatible with the theory tacitly assumed by several of the most important arguments in the *Kritik*. Thus the first defect in the received account is that it is incapable of describing accurately how the distinction between synthetic and analytic judgments functions in Kant's arguments.

What I have singled out as the first major deficiency in the standard account is closely related to another. That account also goes wrong in the interpretation of the character of Kant's distinction between concepts and intuitions. On the standard account, intuitions are not constituents of judgments but are rather perceptual particulars about which we make judgments. The traditional account is, indeed, committed to such a view; for this view is a direct consequence of the prior view that all judgments are exhaustively analyzable into concepts. Given the view that the constituents of a judgment are concepts, then you are bound to deny that intuitions can be logical or semantical entities at all. Here Kant does not supply us with an account of the concept-intuition distinction that forbids us to interpret it as semantical or logical in character. But his avowed doctrine of judgment conflicts with such an interpretation. Yet, if we bracket the avowed theory of judgment and concentrate only on the character of the arguments which Kant gives to make the distinction between concepts and intuitions, what emerges is a new theory of predication —a theory which will be able to explain the reasons for Kant's distinction between analytic and synthetic judgments, not to mention the illumination it casts on the way in which that distinction functions in the major arguments of the *Kritik*.

The standard account is further burdened by a third defect. This concerns the account to be given of the relation between a schematized category and a schema. The problem about this relation grows out of the second claim of the traditional account. The concepts involved in metaphysical propositions are, according to that account, all pure categories. Here Kant supports the claim. For he distinguishes three sets of concepts. There are, first of all, those concepts which Kant calls the functions of thought in judgment. There are, secondly, those concepts which Kant calls the pure categories. And, finally, there are the schematized categories. One thing is clear about this classification: Kant holds that the first two sets are the same concepts. But what is not clear is whether the concepts in the third group I have distinguished are the same as the concepts in the first two groups. Kant does not explicitly say that they are; but he does say this by implication: At B104 he says that the same concepts which give unity to the various representations in a judgment (the first group I have distinguished) give unity to the synthesis of representations in intuition. From this it can be inferred that the concepts involved in the schematized categories are the same as those in the pure categories and the concepts in the functions of thought in judgment. Thus the second claim of the traditional account rests on solid textual foundations: The concepts involved in metaphysical judgments are pure; and this is so even when those concepts are schematized.

But this generates a fundamental difficulty about Kant's view of the way in which a metaphysical proposition must be verified. If you say, as the traditional account does, that the concepts in the schematized categories are pure, then they are compatible with the character of any sensible manifold. For the pure categories yield, as Kant says, only concepts of an object in general—from which it follows that they apply indifferently to phenomena and noumena. There is nothing, that is, that distinguishes the application of these concepts to the

manifold of our sensibility from their application to any other manifold. These concepts will not be concepts of anything in our manifold
which will distinguish it from any other manifold. And it does not
help to say that the pure concepts are limited or restricted by the
schemata to which they are coordinated. For as long as there is
nothing in the concept itself to distinguish its object in our manifold
from the object it would have in any other manifold, then assigning
the concept a schema will only exaggerate the problem: How can we
tell from the pure concept that it is a concept referring to that schema
rather, say, than a schema appropriate to any other sensibility? The
answer is that we cannot. And so long as we cannot do this, there will
be no distinguishing what in our manifold enables us to apply the
pure concepts in metaphysical propositions from what there might be
in any other manifold.

Still less can we remedy this difficulty by supplementing the pure
categories with the *concepts* of the schemata for our sensibility. This
will, to be sure, enable us to distinguish concepts which apply to our
sensibility from those which do not; but it will also have the consequence that the concepts in metaphysical propositions will not be pure
in Kant's sense. For no pure concept contains any mark referring to
intuition. The concepts which would then be called schematized categories would not be the same concepts as the pure categories or the
functions of unity of thought in judgment.

Now this is an issue about which the traditional interpretation, as I
have summarized it, is silent. But it is none the less a defect in that
interpretation if it cannot explain how the concepts in metaphysical
judgments can be pure while still relating to schemata in intuition.
And this defect is just another manifestation of the fundamental
defect in the traditional account—its inability to explain how a concept
relates to an intuition in judgment. As long as it is left unclear how a
concept relates to an intuition, it will remain unclear how a pure
concept can relate to a schema. For it is only by relating to a schema
that such a concept has a relation to intuition. The difficulty I have
just outlined in the relation between pure concepts and schemata is, I

admit, something to which Kant's text itself gives rise. But it is a difficulty that is obscured by the descriptions which Kant gives both of what a judgment is and of the relation of a concept and an intuition in judgment.

There is, finally, a defect which arises out of the fourth claim of the traditional interpretation. But it is just an extension of the difficulty with the relation between pure concepts and schemata. If you hold that the schematized categories are the same concepts as the pure categories, then there will be a problem about explaining how metaphysical propositions, which consist of pure concepts, are verified. The answer which Kant gives to this question is well known: We verify a metaphysical claim by discovering what he calls a third something in virtue of which we justify the combination of the concepts in the metaphysical proposition. The third something in this case is the possibility of experience. But this just perpetuates the difficulty which arose before. If the concepts involved are pure categories, as Kant says they are, there is nothing in our manifold that will justify a combination of them in a metaphysical proposition. The possibility of experience will be, at most, the possibility of experience of an object in general. And this will not tell us how metaphysical propositions make experience of a manifold such as ours possible. It will not do this because what such propositions will make possible is a *thought* of an object in general, which will still not explain how there can be any *objects* in our experience which fall under the pure concepts involved in such propositions. We will not be rescued from this difficulty by saying, as I suggested earlier, that the pure concepts be supplemented by concepts of the schemata in virtue of which they are applied to a manifold such as ours. For this would conflict with Kant's claim that the categories we have are not altered by changes in the kind of manifold we have. Nor will the present difficulty be removed if it is held that the objects in our experience fall under the pure concepts in metaphysical propositions because pure concepts define what it is to be an object in any manifold. It is true that any objects there are in our experience will fall under the concept of an object in general. But this still leaves us ignorant of whether there *are* any such objects which conform to this definition. And whether there are is a question to be answered, not begged.

The difficulty with the verification of metaphysical propositions is mainly exegetical. It results from following the description that Kant himself gives of certain of his arguments. The main problem is in the interpretation of a schematized category: If we hold that the concept here is the same as the corresponding category, the difficulty I have been sketching emerges. Kant's argument demands, as I hope to show, that the schema be, in part, a concept which supplements the concept of the pure category. Although Kant's description of what a schema is does not acknowledge this, the arguments involving the schematized categories assume it. And it is a defect of the traditional account that it does not recognize this.

It should be apparent that none of the difficulties in the traditional account stands alone. The failure to account for how a metaphysical proposition is verified can be traced to the problem of relating schemata to categories. Both of these problems can in turn be traced to the theory of synthetic judgment in Kant. And all of these problems are generated by the problem concerning the concept-intuition distinction. If you are not clear about the status of the distinction between concepts and intuitions, you will not be clear about the constituents of a synthetic proposition and their relation to intuition. And this problem merely concentrates itself in the relation of a pure concept to a schema, unclarity about which will finally render the explication of such notions as the possibility of experience or the third thing in a metaphysical judgment a quixotic adventure condemned to confusion.

This will conclude my criticism of the received account of Kant's program in metaphysics. Since it is only partly supported by the *Kritik,* resulting mainly from reading Kant's arguments only through the spectacles which are supplied by Kant's reflective statements about them, I shall contrast it with another account of his program which is supported by the way in which he argues and which is free from the difficulties of the received account. What I shall argue, then, is that the Kantian program actually has the following character:

1′. Most metaphysical propositions are synthetic. They are not composed of concepts alone but rather of concepts and intuitions: A metaphysical proposition that is synthetic asserts that intuitions fall under concepts, not that one concept is related to another.

2′. What makes a proposition metaphysical is the kind of concept involved in metaphysical propositions. But there are two kinds of metaphysical proposition. There is, first, the kind that involves unschematized categories and which is analytic of the concept of an object in general. There is, secondly, the kind that involves schematized categories. The latter kind of proposition is synthetic because it relates an intuition to a concept. The concept is a schematized category, while the intuition is a transcendental schema.

3′. Metaphysical propositions that are synthetic are verified by reference to a third thing, which is the intuition falling under the schematized concept. The third thing for such propositions is a transcendental schema.

4′. The possibility of experience is a transcendental schema. The schema is the necessary condition of our experience of objects, for the schema is two things, not one. It is part of the category; and it is the referent of that category in intuition.

I have formulated my claims so that 1′–4′ can be set in sharp contrast to 1–4. The evidence which supports this rather than the traditional view of Kant's position is mainly indirect, depending as it does upon the contrast between many of the arguments of the *Kritik* and Kant's description of those arguments. The main issue between those adopting the traditional view and those adopting the view for which I shall be arguing is the interpretation of the concept-intuition distinction. Acceptance of Kant's account of the theory of judgment in the *Kritik* will almost surely prevent one from seeing any of the other problems about the verification of metaphysical propositions. Both Chapter Two and Chapter Three of this book will help to establish the presence of two theories of predication in the *Kritik*. Here I shall try to show that Kant adopted a theory of predication from the logical tradition which could not be accommodated to the distinction he draws between concepts and intuitions. Thus we have two different theories. One is the theory which Kant inherited from the tradition and used to expound his distinction between synthetic and analytic propositions. The other is the theory which is presupposed by many of the arguments in the *Kritik* and which is demanded by Kant's way of distinguishing between concepts and intuitions.

Chapter Four continues the argument by an analysis of Kant's theory of schematism. If we accept the view, defended in the first and second chapters, that synthetic propositions are combinations, not of two concepts, but of a concept and an intuition, the problem will arise of finding an intuition which is combined with a pure category in the synthetic propositions of metaphysics. The kinds of intuition which are combined with pure categories are transcendental schemata. Appealing to the chapter on schematism in the *Kritik* to support any theory is, to be sure, like appealing to the Cumaean Sibyl. So my use of that chapter to confirm my thesis will be preceded by an elimination of the other interpretations to which that chapter has lent itself in the past.

Chapter Five carries the general line of argument concerning Kant's theory of synthetic *a priori* propositions to the first and second Analogies. Here I propose to take my theory of Kant's synthetic *a priori* and show that it can explain the kind of argument which he gives for two paradigm cases of metaphysical propositions. Thus I shall argue that, in both the arguments which he gives in the Analogies, Kant is showing that the concepts of substance and causation have intuitions corresponding to them in our sensibility. The interpretation for which I shall argue not only fits the general view I take of what the synthetic *a priori* is for Kant but has the additional advantage of explaining, as other accounts cannot, why Kant should have separated the chapter on schematism from the arguments he gives for the Analogies and why, after having proved that our manifold must be subject to the pure concepts of the understanding, he none the less goes on to offer separate proofs for the application of each of those concepts.

Chapter Five concludes the major exegetical task of this book. What I defend through that chapter is the exegetical adequacy of the view of the synthetic *a priori* that I attribute to Kant. In Chapter Six I take up the relation of metaphysical propositions as Kant understands them to the Transcendental Method. This chapter will mark a departure from the line of argument which unified the antecedent chapters. In those chapters I am concerned to arrive at an account of Kant's notion of the synthetic *a priori* that is exegetically adequate. It is this account, particularly as it is illustrated in the first and second Analogies, that I find inadequate as a philosophical theory of metaphysical propositions. This is what dictates the structure of the final chapter. There I begin by asking whether the conditions which Kant places on the practice of the Transcendental Method enable us to reconstruct a theory of the synthetic *a priori* in metaphysics which is free from the kinds of difficulties which attend the examples Kant gives of that kind of proposition in the first and second Analogies. But Kant himself left the general characteristics of the Transcendental Method largely unformulated; and this has provoked a number of accounts of what the method is which must be eliminated before an attempt can be made to formulate the conditions of the method more accurately. Thus the first task of Chapter Six is to distinguish four different accounts of that method which have been offered or which might easily be offered and to show that they fail either because they conflict with other things Kant holds or because the attribution of them to Kant would leave large gaps in his argument. The formulation of the method which I shall defend as adequate to Kant's practice divides that method into a substantive claim about what counts as a properly metaphysical concept and a form of argument by which it can be shown whether any such concept has instances or not. And I shall argue that the viability of Kant's notion of the synthetic *a priori* in metaphysics depends upon his ability to defend the substantive claim about what counts as a metaphysical concept.

There remains only one thing to be remarked upon because it will no doubt appear to many, as it has already appeared to some, as an irony of procedure. The book argues throughout that Kant has lent himself to misinterpretation; and one of the principal tools used to show that such a misinterpretation is in fact present is that consequences can be deduced from the interpretation that conflict with other things Kant says. And yet, the interpretation which I defend appears to have the same defect: It departs from the apparent meaning of the text only to show that, in the end, the doctrine it interprets is defective. But is this not reason enough to reject it as an interpretation? Or, at the very least, is it not enough to invalidate the grounds on which I reject what I have called the traditional account of Kant's doctrine?

The sense of irony here is, at best, an inarticulate commentary about laboring so long over a philosophical text the doctrine of which must, in part, be found inadequate. But it is no genuine objection to the standards of proof used in the exegesis of that text. One prima facie reason for rejecting any reading of a text is that it conflicts with other things the author says. This is, of course, not a foolproof exegetical device. If it were, then it would be logically impossible for any author to contradict himself. But it is, at least, an admissible one if another reading can be constructed to remove the conflict. This is very different from raising philosophical difficulties about a text. And while showing that an interpretation entails a philosophical difficulty does constitute a reason for doubting it, such a conclusion alone is never enough to reject the interpretation. The interpretation of Kant I reject has the defect both of conflicting with other things Kant says and of entailing philosophical difficulties. The interpretation of Kant which I defend entails only, I believe, that the doctrine has certain philosophical difficulties.

CHAPTER TWO

Kant and the Problem

of Predication

ARLY IN THE *Kritik* Kant introduces a distinction which, he tells us, he was the first in the history of philosophy to advance. He says that there are two relations of concepts in a judgment:

> Either the predicate B belongs to the subject A, as something which is (covertly) contained in this concept A; or B lies outside the concept A, although it does indeed stand in connection with it. In the one case I entitle the judgment analytic, in the other synthetic.[1]

Here Kant makes a break with the tradition: He holds that there are true judgments in which the predicate concept lies outside the subject concept. But what is baffling about this break is why Kant should have

1. A6 = B10.

thought that it was demanded. The usual explanation is to say that
the distinction was discovered by Kant and that it had eluded logical
theorists before him. Kemp Smith puts it this way:

> Kant's Critical problem arose from the startling discovery that the *a priori*
> and the synthetic do not exclude one another. . . . He appears to have made
> this discovery under the influence of Hume, through study of the general
> principle of causality—every event must have a cause. In that judgment there
> seems to be no connection of any kind discoverable between the subject (the
> conception of an event as something happening in time) and the predicate
> (the conception of another event preceding it as an originating cause); and
> yet we not merely ascribe the one to the other but assert that they are
> necessarily connected.[2]

This is faithful to the way in which Kant introduces his new distinction in the *Kritik:* He gives examples of propositions that are true
and still synthetic. I do not here propose to take up the examples he
offers of such propositions. All I shall presently argue is that, if we
take this characterization of Kant's discovery seriously, we will not be
able to find out just what he was opposing in the tradition or how he
should have thought that there were any such propositions.

The first unsettling thing about the foregoing description is that it
appears to be compatible with a totally different inference. There is,
Kant holds, a large class of propositions which are synthetic but about
which we can know that the subject and predicate concepts are universally and necessarily combined. But why is this not reason enough to
justify the inference that the predicate concept in such propositions is,
after all, contained in the subject concept? Here Kant appeals to what
we do or do not think in the subject concept: We do not, for example,
think the concept of "having a cause" in our concept of "event." And
yet, Kant also holds that these concepts are universally and necessarily true of experience. But how does he distinguish the way in which
these concepts are universally and necessarily true of experience from
the way in which the concepts of "man" and "rational animal" are
universally and necessarily true of experience when they are combined

---

2. Norman Kemp Smith, *A Commentary to Kant's* Critique of Pure
Reason (New York: Humanities Press, 1962), p. 30.

in the analytic proposition, "All men are rational animals"? The failure to find an exception in experience to a proposition has the defect of rendering it impossible to distinguish between analytic and synthetic *a priori* propositions. The only grounds on which one could make the distinction, then, would be the results of what we do and do not think in the subject concept of the proposition in question. But such an appeal can easily be invalidated once it is shown that there is a compelling reason for regarding synthetic *a priori* propositions as analytic.

But there is something else that is unsettling about the description Kant gives to the distinction between synthetic and analytic propositions. The examples which he gives in the Introduction to the *Kritik* are all synthetic *a priori* propositions. And yet, he extends the distinction he is introducing to synthetic *a posteriori* propositions. These are all propositions the truth or falsity of which is made out by an appeal to the facts of experience which they describe. Yet why should they be thought to be synthetic? The answer Kant would give to this question would, I believe, be this:

> Judgments of experience, as such, are one and all synthetic. For it would be absurd to found an analytic judgment on experience. Since, in framing the judgment, I must not go outside my concept, there is no need to appeal to the testimony of experience in its support.[3]

But this is a strange reason to think that judgments of experience cannot be analytic. A judgment could be analytic and still tell us something about experience. There may, to be sure, be a good reason why this is not the case. But the description of such a possibility is still not obviously self-contradictory. So it may indeed be absurd to found an analytic judgment on experience; but it does not follow that what are judgments about experience cannot be analytic in Kant's sense.

This point can be made somewhat differently, as follows. I am claiming that Kant moves from saying that a judgment is a judgment *of* experience to the conclusion that such a judgment is a judgment *about* experience. For he first says that the results of consulting

3. A7 = B11.

experience are always formulated in synthetic judgments. He then says that any proposition whose truth can be ascertained without going outside the internal structure of the proposition is analytic. And Kant takes it to follow from this that analytic propositions cannot be judgments of experience. He also takes it to follow that no analytic proposition can be about experience. For knowing that a proposition is about experience is knowing something more than can be discovered by an examination of the proposition itself. This is the reason why Kant believes that all judgments which are about experience are synthetic. What is strange about this is why a fact about the relation between a proposition and experience should be construed as a fact about the internal structure of the proposition. To say of a judgment, as Kant does, that it is about experience does not permit an immediate inference to anything concerning the relation which the concepts in the proposition have to each other. Why, then, should Kant have thought that all judgments of experience must be synthetic rather than analytic?

There are, then, two facts that make it very difficult to understand either why Kant did think he had good reason to break with the tradition of logical theory or why we should take this break seriously. What is wrong here is the characterization Kant gives of the break he is making. And I shall argue that both of the difficulties which can be raised with the break as he describes it can be removed once the distinction between synthetic and analytic judgments is drawn, not by following the description Kant gives, but by seeing that the distinction he draws demands, not merely an alteration of the relation of concepts in a true judgment, but a new theory of predication.

⟨ I ⟩

The Relevance of Kant's Immediate Predecessors:
An Obstacle Removed

THE FIRST STEP toward understanding the character of Kant's new distinction between synthetic and analytic judgments is to see it in contrast to the theory of predication as held in the tradition before Kant. The view of predication with which Kant's distinction invites comparison is Leibniz'; for Leibniz held that there can be no true synthetic propositions. And since this is precisely what Kant denied, it would seem that the theory Kant is offering is erected on a rejection of the Leibnizian view. But this would be a mistake. Kant did, of course, reject the view, held by Leibniz, that all true propositions must be analytic. But this rejection would be significant only if Leibniz had propounded a theory according to which there could be analytic propositions about this world as distinct from all possible worlds. And since, as I hope to show, Leibniz' theory did not permit him to hold this, the theory he did hold is merely absorbed by Kant's theory and, for that reason, cannot be significantly contrasted with it.

Let us consider the part of Leibniz' theory that shows this. The fundamental claim is that the predicate of every true, affirmative proposition is contained in the notion of its subject. Thus Leibniz says: "In consulting the notion which I have of every true proposition, I find that every predicate, necessary or contingent, past, present, or future, is comprised in the notion of the subject . . ." [4] To say of a proposition that it is false, then, is just to say that it asserts of a subject what does not belong to it. If a predicate does not belong to the subject of which it is asserted, then it is not contained in the notion of the subject. From this Leibniz infers that to say a predicate does belong to a subject is to say that it is part of the notion of the subject.

There is an immediate consequence of this theory: The only difference between necessary truth and contingent truth is that the latter requires an infinite analysis for the discovery that the predicate is contained in the notion of the subject. Leibniz recognizes this when he says:

The difference between necessary and contingent truths is indeed the same as that between commensurable and incommensurable numbers. For the reduction of commensurable numbers to a common measure is analogous to the demonstration of necessary truths, or their reduction to such as are identical.

4. C. I. Gerhardt, *Die philosophischen Schriften von G. W. Leibniz* (Berlin: Weidmann, 1875–90), II, 46; cf. VII, 199.

But as, in the case of surd ratios, the reduction involves an infinite process, and yet approaches a common measure, so that a definite but unending series is obtained, so also contingent truths require an infinite analysis, which God alone can accomplish.[5]

The distinction between necessary and contingent truths does not, however, alter the cornerstone of Leibniz' theory of predication: Even a contingent truth meets the requirement that its predicate be contained in the notion of the subject.

But let us ask what, on Leibniz' theory, a true proposition is about. The answer that comes to mind is that a contingent truth is about a fact in a particular world while a necessary truth is about a fact in all possible worlds. That a necessary truth is about a fact in all possible worlds is recognized by Leibniz when he says that, "as for eternal truths, we must observe that at bottom they are all hypothetical, and say in fact: such a thing posited, such another thing is." [6] If a proposition is true hypothetically, there will be no possible world in which a state of affairs would exclude it. And it would not be excluded from any possible world simply because such a truth is compatible with the truth of any proposition in every logically possible world. This can be shown as follows. A necessary proposition is true in any possible world you specify. If it were not, then a state of affairs would *ex hypothesi* obtain in the possible world in which such a proposition does not obtain that would have a self-contradictory description; hence, the proposition is true in all possible worlds.

This entails a consequence for Leibniz' theory of contingent propositions which prevents the theory as a whole from being contrasted with Kant's. A contingent truth is like a necessary truth in that both have their predicate concepts contained in the notion of the subject. But if this is so, then it follows that even a contingent proposition is true in all possible worlds. To say that a contingent proposition is true is to say that its denial generates a contradiction. But if the denial of

5. *Ibid.*, IV, 438–39, quoted in Nicholas Rescher, *The Philosophy of Leibniz* (Englewood Cliffs, N.J.: Prentice-Hall, 1967), p. 38 n.
6. Gerhardt, *op. cit.*, V, 428; cf. pp. 414 and 429.

such a proposition generates a contradiction, it follows that the original proposition must be true in all possible worlds. For a proposition is true in this way only if the choice of a world in which it would be false would give us a self-contradictory description as part of the total description of the possible world. Hence it follows that both necessary and contingent propositions are about the same thing; namely, all possible worlds.

But why is this theory of predication not susceptible of contrast with the theory presupposed by Kant's distinction between analytic and synthetic judgments? The reason is that the entirety of Leibniz' theory is absorbed into Kant's theory of analytic propositions. What for Leibniz counts as the totality of possible worlds appears in Kant's theory as an object in general. Thus Kant says that the unschematized categories apply to an object in general: They apply to any kind of object indifferently.[7] And this is true of any proposition which, on Kant's theory, is analytic. Kant says that "the Understanding in its analytic employment is concerned only to know what lies in the concept; it is indifferent as to the object to which the concept may apply."[8] For this reason there is nothing internal to Leibniz' theory of predication that permits a contrast with Kant's. It is true, of course, that there is a disagreement about whether there can be true synthetic propositions. But that is a disagreement about the adequacy of the theory Leibniz offers to certain cases of predication. It is not an issue internal to the theory; hence, Kant's theory cannot be significantly contrasted with the theory that Leibniz offers.

2

The Leibnizian Theory Revised

ALTHOUGH THERE WAS NOT A GENUINE CONTRAST between the Leibnizian theory as it was stated above and Kant's new alternative, such a

7. B128; B150; A289 = B346; A247 = B304.
8. A259 = B315.

contrast can be made once either of two premises in Leibniz' theory is modified or abandoned. The premises are these: (1) that all necessary propositions are true in all possible worlds; and (2) that contingent propositions are reducible to necessary propositions. I see no way of altering (2) short of forcing the abandonment of the cornerstone of Leibniz' theory of predication. Once you hold, for example, that there is a difference in kind between necessary and contingent truths, you can no longer hold that the denial of every true proposition entails a contradiction. And this is tantamount to giving up the entire theory of predication. There is a way, however, of altering (1) without abandoning the theory of predication on which it rests. It is possible to hold that at least some necessary propositions are categorical. This would, of course, conflict with Leibniz' claim that all necessary propositions are hypothetical. But it is possible to state this alteration in a way that would not make that conflict seem so blatant. Leibniz does hold—whether consistently or not—that there is a difference between necessary and contingent propositions. Thus it would be quite possible to maintain that all propositions whose subject concepts are individual notions and thus refer to individual substances are contingent and categorical. In this way it does not follow that all necessary propositions are hypothetical. For although even propositions whose subject concepts are individual notions would be ultimately necessary if true, the modification just suggested would prevent them from becoming hypothetical.

There is, moreover, evidence that Leibniz would assent to such a view. At one place he says this:

All contingent propositions have sufficient reasons, or, equivalently, have *a priori* proofs which establish their certainty, and which show that the connection of subject and predicate of these propositions has its foundation in their nature. But it is not the case that contingent propositions have demonstrations of necessity, since their sufficient reasons are based on the principle of contingence or of the existence of things, i.e., on what is or seems the best among equally possible alternatives, while necessary truths are founded upon the principle of contradictions and [on that] of the possibility or impossibility of the essences themselves, without having regard in that respect on the free will of God or of creatures.[9]

Here Leibniz distinguishes between propositions the truth of which depends upon the existence of the subject and those which do not presuppose that their subjects exist. The former would include what on the revised theory I suggested are propositions about individual substances. One of the truth conditions of such propositions would be the existence of the subject. And this would separate such propositions from necessary propositions properly so called. In this way (1) can be modified. For propositions about individual substances would not be true in all possible worlds because it is not self-contradictory to deny the existence of any created substance.

This, then, is the revised theory. And it brings the Leibnizian theory into direct conflict with Kant's claim that there are true synthetic propositions. On the Leibnizian theory, there are necessary propositions that are not true in all possible worlds. For even though propositions about individual substances are not hypothetical, their predicates are still contained in their subject concepts. And the denial of such a proposition still entails a contradiction, even though it takes a divine analyst to exhibit that contradiction.

But just how does Kant break with this theory? The argument which enables Kant to break with this theory will show that the following are mutually exclusive claims:

The predicates of propositions about individuals are contained in the expression serving as the subject concept of those propositions.

The subject expressions of such propositions designate individuals.

That these claims are indeed mutually exclusive does not follow from Kant's theory as he describes it. But such a conclusion does follow from the distinction he makes between concepts and intuitions. And that, irrespective of the description Kant gives, this conclusion is meant to follow from the concept-intuition distinction will be the burden of the following section.

9. Gerhardt, *op. cit.*, IV, 438–39, quoted in Rescher, *op. cit.*, p. 38 n.

❁ 3 ❁

Concepts and Intuitions: The Traditional View

KANT HIMSELF DOES NOT CLAIM that the distinction between concepts and intuitions demands a new theory of predication. The theory of predication which he claims to have succeeds only in ignoring the importance of that distinction for predication. The first step in showing how that distinction is the basis of a theory of predication is to show why the traditional account is false. Kemp Smith offers what has become the received interpretation. Beginning with Kant's remark that an intuition is a kind of knowledge that relates immediately to an object, Smith holds that "intuition" is a term that Kant uses "to cover sensations of all the senses." [10] And Smith holds the same view elsewhere when he says that "the immediate object of the intuition is a sense-content, which Kant, following the universally accepted view of the time, regards as purely subjective." [11] One thing is clear about this account of what an intuition is: It is incompatible with the view that the distinction between intuition and concept holds between two entities in judgment. For once you interpret an intuition as an item in the mental history of the percipient, then, so far from forming a new theory of predication, the distinction is compatible with any theory of predication at all.

But what is the evidence for interpreting an intuition as Kemp

---

10. Kemp Smith, *op. cit.*, p. 79; here Kemp Smith does say that space and time are forms of sensation, leaving it open whether they are sensations themselves. Yet the position in this passage implies that space and time are sensations once it is taken in connection with what Kant says at B160: "But space and time are represented *a priori* not merely as *forms* of sensible intuition, but as themselves *intuitions* which contain a manifold of their own." H. J. Paton, *Kant's Metaphysic of Experience* (2 vols.; London: George Allen & Unwin, 1951), I, 97, has the same view when he says: "Intuition itself may be analyzed into form and matter. The matter is the sensation or sensum, which may also be called an impression. This is the 'effect' of the object which 'affects' our minds. The form is the space and time in which sensations are arranged."

11. Kemp Smith, *op. cit.*, p. 80.

Smith does? There are, first of all, passages in which Kant allegedly holds this view outright. The principal passage occurs at A20 = B34, where Kant says, according to Kemp Smith, that "it is also through sensation that empirical intuition acquires its object, i.e., *that sensation is the content of intuition*." [12] And there are other passages in which Kant refers to intuition as "the subjective condition of sensibility," "lying ready in our minds," and "necessarily preceding [as the form of the subject's receptivity] all intuitions of objects." [13]

But this textual evidence does not support the conclusion that Kemp Smith seeks to draw from it. Consider, for example, Kant's claim that sensation is the content of intuition. What this shows is, not that sensation *is* intuition, but at most that sensation invariably accompanies intuition. And sensations can invariably accompany intuition without being identical with it. The same point can be made for the family of locutions, cited by Kemp Smith, by which Kant apparently speaks of intuitions as subjective. All of these locutions are, at the very least, too ambiguous to give support to Kemp Smith's interpretation. To say that something is the subjective condition of sensibility does not yield the conclusion that it is mental. For such a claim is compatible with the conclusion that the condition in question is indispensable for us without therefore being an item in our mental history. The same ambiguity is present, although less obviously, in the phrase, "lying ready in our minds." Something could have this status by being the necessary condition of mental activity of a certain kind without being a property of that activity.

But worse is to come. What is wrong with the view that Kemp Smith takes is not merely that the premises used to establish it are ambiguous. There are other passages which forbid such an interpretation. At A320 Kant gives the following classification of ideas or representations:

The genus is *representation* in general (*repraesentio*). Subordinate to it stands representation with consciousness (*perceptio*). A *perception* which relates solely to the subject as a modification of its state is sensation (*sensatio*),

12. *Ibid.*, p. 82.
13. *Ibid.*, p. 103.

an objective perception is *knowledge* (*cognitio*). This is either *intuition or concept* (*intuitus vel conceptus*). The former relates immediately to the object and is single, the latter refers to it mediately by means of a feature which several things have in common.[14]

Intuitions are objective in that they are independent of the individual mental histories of a group of percipients. Sensations are never independent in this way. And so, if Kant had taken an intuition to be a sensation, he could not have distinguished in this way between objective perceptions and perceptions relating to the subject alone.

There is another passage in which Kant is committed to rejecting the equation of sensations and intuitions. At B274–79 he argues that representations of one's own existence presuppose the existence of objects in space outside me. The conclusion of that argument runs like this:

Thus perception of this permanent is possible only through a *thing* outside me; and consequently the determination of my own existence in time is possible only through the existence of actual things which I perceive outside me.[15]

I am not concerned here with the truth or falsity of this conclusion but only with one of its presuppositions. Such a conclusion implies that I must be aware of certain things in my experience which are not merely modifications of my subjective state. And this in turn is incompatible with the view according to which intuitions are sensations. For if intuitions were sensations, then the conclusion for which Kant is arguing here would be impossible to establish. Thus the conclusion presupposes that there are some intuitions that are not sensations. It is still, to be sure, an open question whether I do in fact ever perceive anything but sensations; and, in this passage, Kant argues that we do. But whether the argument is successful does not affect the presupposition that it must be at least logically possible to perceive in intuition something other than sensations. And that it is logically possible to do this shows that an intuition cannot by definition be a sensation.

There is, then, textual evidence for the conclusion that intuitions

14. Cf. Kant's *Logik*, para. 1 (*Werke*, VIII, 88–89).
15. B275.

are not identical with sensations. But there is an equally telling objection to the received interpretation of an intuition: The assumption that Kant held it entails consequences that contradict other things he says. If we hold that intuitions are items in our mental history, then it would follow that both space and time would be subjective, since they are both contents of intuition as well as forms of intuition.[16] But if this is so, then Kant can no longer distinguish things in inner from things in outer sense. What is mental or purely subjective is for Kant temporal but not spatial; what is physical is both spatial and temporal. For time is the form of inner sense, while space is the form of outer sense.[17] But if all intuitions are subjective, then we are left with the contradiction that space both is and is not the form of outer sense. To say that space is the form of outer sense is to say that things in space are not subjective: They are not merely items in our mental history. But to say that space is an intuition would, on this view, be to say that it is subjective; and this would entail that it is only an item in inner sense. That is the contradiction.

This embarrassment for the received interpretation cannot, it should be noted, be removed by an appeal to the distinction between transcendental ideality and empirical reality. It might be said, for example, that intuitions are mental only in that they are transcendentally ideal, not in the sense that they are empirically ideal. Thus space might be said to be nothing for us outside our representation while still not being a purely subjective affection of the percipient.[18] But this attempt to rescue the present account of intuition only has to be articulated to be declared a failure. As long as one says that intuitions, including space and time, are sensations, then it is not open to one to say that they are subjective only in the sense that they are nothing for us outside our experience. For this sense is ambiguous just where clarity is demanded: If intuitions are subjective only in that they are nothing for us outside our experience, then it does not follow that they are subjective affections of the percipient; and then it no longer

16. B160.
17. A26–34 = B42–50.
18. Cf. A369 ff. and A376 ff.

follows that intuitions are sensations. If transcendental ideality is then narrowed to mean that they are purely subjective, the notion of transcendental ideality would be nothing more than a new designation for the same difficulty that it was introduced to remove.

There remains only one more consequence to be drawn from the traditional interpretation of Kant's doctrine of intuition. We are assuming for the sake of argument that space, like any other intuition, is a sensation. On this assumption it would follow that an impression or sense content, which is unextended, is really extended. An impression can be dated. It can be given a temporal location in our mental history. But a sensation cannot be given spatial coordinates. To give a spatial location to a sensation is to assign it a place which is open to the observation of others. And in that case an impression would no longer be merely a modification of one's own state. It would be an item of experience for others as well. It would, accordingly, cease to be an impression as both Kant and Kemp Smith understand that word. So, given that understanding of what a sensation is, such an entity cannot be localized in space.[19] But if we hold that space is a sensation, then it would follow that something extended would either not be extended—which gives us a contradiction—or that some impressions are, after all, extended—which gives us another contradiction. And this is the conclusion to which the view that an intuition is a sensation or sense impression logically commits those who hold it. This conclusion is not itself sufficient to prove that Kant did not hold the doctrine in question. But it does make it highly unlikely that Kant should have held a theory that leads immediately to such an absurd conclusion.

The traditional account of an intuition must, then, be pronounced a failure. My reason for rejecting what I have called the traditional account is not that it lacks *all* foundation in Kant's text. What is wrong with the traditional account is that it purports to be the whole exegetical story about intuitions. Thus Kemp Smith and Paton are surely right when they say that, in Kant's view, intuitions are those

19. A sensation can, of course, be assigned to a part of one's body. But that is the *seat* of the sensation as distinct from the sensation itself.

things which result from the effects upon our sensibility produced by objects outside us. But this is not the only way in which Kant thought about intuitions, and it is incompatible with the assumptions he makes about the character of intuitions in some of the arguments in the *Kritik*. And the traditional account cannot be rescued from the problems surrounding it by having it pointed out, as both Kemp Smith and Paton do, that the sensationalist view of intuitions applies only to empirical intuition, while space and time, being the *forms* of intuition, are not sensations. This will not help the traditional view for two reasons. For one thing, anybody holding that view would be forced to extend it to the forms of intuition themselves just because Kant himself holds that the forms of intuition are themselves intuitions. For another, the forms of intuition share the property of subjectivity in common with empirical intuitions. And this is the property which makes the sensationalist interpretation of intuitions so objectionable. For it runs counter to the way in which Kant thinks about intuitions in the passages in the *Kritik* which I have been discussing. Once you link empirical intuitions and the forms of intuition in virtue of their subjectivity, forms of intuition are just sensations under a different name.

§4

Concepts and Intuitions:
Some Objectionable Alternative Views

BUT IF INTUITIONS ARE NOT SENSATIONS or sense impressions, what are they? There is little to help us here in Kant's descriptions of intuitions. When he tells us what an intuition is, he says variously that it is what we receive through sensibility and that it is a singular idea.[20] But this is incompatible only with the view that we are given universals through sensibility; and it is compatible with any view of an intuition as long as that view recognizes that intuitions are individuals. The

---

20. Cf. A19 = B33; *Logik*, para. 1 (*Werke*, VIII, 88–89).

solution to this problem is, first, to state the argument by which Kant shows that there is a distinction between intuitions and concepts and, secondly, to ask what kind of distinction can be inferred from it.

The argument for that distinction is given at A25 for space and at A32 for time. I shall restrict my attention here to the argument for space, since the form of that argument can be easily extended to cover time. It runs like this. There are, we are told, two reasons for distinguishing between space on the one hand and concepts on the other. Space can be represented only as a whole of parts. Thus any given spatial volume will itself be a part of a larger spatial volume. Concepts cannot be represented this way. The division of a concept will not yield concepts that are quantitative parts of a more inclusive concept.

The argument assumes, as it stands, another step. It assumes that the division of a concept will yield an entity of a different kind, while division performed on space will not. And it is easy to see that this is true. When I divide a volume of space, the result is always a smaller volume of the same space. When I divide the concept, say, of brother, the result is the concept of a different thing: either the concept of male or that of sibling.

The second reason for distinguishing between space and concepts is this. The parts of space do not precede the whole of which they are parts. The constituents of concepts do precede the complex concept of which they are parts. The use of "precedes" here is clearly logical. Both the concepts of male and sibling are logically prior to the concept of brother. But separate volumes of space do not logically precede space itself, although they in part constitute space. The crucial distinction here is that between two senses of "limitation." One concept limits another only by restricting the class of objects which fall under it. But one volume of space cannot limit another in this way. Space is limited by one of its parts only in that the part is included by a larger whole. And this explains why the parts of space cannot precede space. To say this would be to say that a limitation, which presupposes the whole of which it is a limitation in order to exist, precedes that whole. Thus it would be contradictory to say that parts of space logically precede the whole of which they are limitations.

This argument gives Kant the conclusion that there are two kinds of representations, singular and general. The word which makes trouble is "representation": We can take it to mean either the object of an act of representing, the content of such an act, or the act itself. Here Kant must be taken to mean, at least, that the representation of something singular is different from that of something general just because, although they are both acts, they differ in what they represent. Thus the third way of interpreting "representation," although admissible, would be irrelevant to the question of what the distinction is between the two kinds of things which are represented. Thus only the first two alternatives are relevant here. The distinction between intuitions and concepts holds between the objects of the act of representing or it holds between the content of such acts. The distinction that I introduce here between the content and the object of representation is unproblematic. For all I intend to mark here is the distinction between the expression stating what is represented and the object to which that expression refers. The former can be true or false; the latter cannot. And this is no more than the distinction which Kant himself introduces when he says, at A58 = B82, that truth is the agreement of knowledge with its object. And given the further premise that knowledge consists in judgments, the conclusion is just the distinction between a judgment, which I have called the content of representation, and the object, which is what that content is about.[21]

There are, then, the following alternatives in understanding the distinction between concepts and intuitions:

1. Intuitions are objects of perception while concepts are what enable us to apprehend these objects.
2. Intuitions are objects of thought while concepts are the way in which we apprehend these objects.

---

21. Cf. A68 = B93; *Nachlass*, Nos. 4638 and 5923 (in *Kant's Gesammelte Schriften*, edited by the Prussian Academy of Science [24 vols.; Berlin and Leipzig: Walter de Gruyter, from 1910]. All *Nachlass* numbers refer to Vol. XVI of this edition).

3. Intuitions are individuals and concepts are common properties.
4. Intuitions are expressions for individuals and concepts are predicates in judgments.

The first and second of these alternatives treat the distinction as that between a content of representation and the object of that content. The third alternative treats the distinction as that between two kinds of objects. And the fourth treats it as a distinction between two kinds of elements in the content of representation. Let us take these alternatives in turn.

Consider the first alternative. If we take this view of the distinction, then the argument for that distinction which I summarized above would show that an intuition is a perceptual particular which we grasp when we apply concepts to perceptual experience. And the point of the distinction would be to show that a perceptual particular is different from the means by which we apprehend it. But this way of looking at the distinction cannot be right. What it requires us to do is to take Kant's argument as showing that there is a distinction between thought and its characteristics on the one hand and the characteristics of the perceptual objects which thought is about on the other. An intuition for Kant is, of course, perceptual: That is just a consequence of the definition of "intuition." But the argument by which Kant distinguishes intuitions from concepts can be taken to show this only if we are willing to say that the conclusion of the argument has nothing to do with the premises.

There are two reasons for this. (1) What Kant's argument for distinguishing between concepts and intuitions proves is that intuitions are representations which differ in kind from concepts. They are different representations. But this argument is completely silent about whether intuitions are perceptual particulars and thus require concepts in order to be represented. That what is given to us through intuition is also an object of representation is the consequence of Kant's claim that pure intuition is the form of all empirical intuition. Yet this is not a conclusion of Kant's argument for the distinction between intuitions and concepts. And that argument does not prove that intuitions require concepts in order to be represented. (2) The present interpretation requires us to look upon Kant's argument as showing that concepts are mental while intuitions are not: A concept is that through which a mind makes contact with an intuition; an intuition is not a characteristic of a concept. For it is given independently of the existence of concepts. But you can accept Kant's argument at A25 and A32 and still be completely uncommitted about whether intuitions are mental. Whether they are mental is decided by Kant only by the very different argument he gives at A24. And so it is possible to accept the conclusions of the argument by which Kant distinguishes between concepts and intuitions while remaining silent about whether concepts are mental and whether intuitions are what is cognized by concepts. Thus the present interpretation of the concept-intuition distinction has the defect of making the argument for that distinction irrelevant to its conclusion.

The second alternative does not fare much better than the first. All it claims is that the distinction is between an object which is thought and the concepts by which we recognize that object in thought. Thus the notion of a particular has been expanded. What counts as a particular is no longer that which is presented in perception but whatever can be brought before the mind and contemplated as an object. But this possibility is even less fortunate than the first one. For this interpretation would entail the breakdown of the entire distinction between concepts and intuitions. A concept would have to be counted as an intuition once it is made an object of thought. So this interpretation of Kant's argument is inadmissible because it entails the collapse of the very distinction which the argument was intended to make.

The failure of the first two alternatives teaches us a valuable lesson: Kant's argument for the distinction between concepts and intuitions cannot be taken as an argument to distinguish between an object of thought or perception and the means by which we apprehend that object. But this leaves another possibility open. Perhaps Kant's argument establishes the conclusion that intuitions are particulars and that concepts are common properties shared by many intuitions. This is the third alternative mentioned above. And if it is right, it would require us to construe the distinction as obtaining between elements in the object or representation. The argument would, accordingly, show that intuitions are neither constructed out of concepts nor contain concepts as parts; and it would show that concepts are properties common to many intuitions.

Kant's argument for the distinction between concepts and intuitions does, it should be noted, establish that intuitions cannot be constructed out of sets of concepts. What Kant shows is that there are certain characteristics which intuitions simply would not have if they were to be so constructed. They would not, for example, be divisible in the way they are if they were constructed out of concepts. And this shows that such a construction could not be carried out. But to show that an individual cannot be constructed out of concepts is not to show that concepts and intuitions are elements in the perceptual objects given in intuition. You can agree with the conclusion that intuitions cannot be constructed out of concepts and still make no commitments about the existence of common properties. You can hold, for example, that common properties are numerically identical through their various instantiations, or that they are only qualitatively identical, or even that they do not exist at all. And any of these positions would be compatible with the conclusion that intuitions cannot be constructed out of concepts. But if this is so, then the argument Kant gives to distinguish between concepts and intuitions is not an argument showing that concepts and intuitions are irreducible elements or components in the perceptual object. Such a conclusion is irrelevant to the premises of that argument; hence, the same defect vitiates the third alternative that beset the first and second alternatives.

This argument cannot, however, go without qualification. When I say that Kant's argument for the concept-intuition distinction does not mark out a distinction between two parts or constituents of a perceptual object, I do not mean that, for Kant, there is no distinction between things and their properties. The fact is that I think that Kant's argument can be used to establish the irreducible difference between the two. The only thing I wish to deny is that this is the only thing the argument establishes. Thus my point in showing that the argument is compatible with any theory of properties is that it cannot legitimately be taken to establish something solely about perceptual objects. What the argument establishes is something about the distinction between a concept—as distinct from a property—and an intuition. This is enough to show that the force of the argument cannot be restricted to the elements of a perceptual object, although it may legitimately be taken to have consequences for the constituents of those objects.

I conclude that none of the foregoing alternatives is an accurate interpretation of Kant's argument. The character of this conclusion must not be misconstrued. To show, as I have tried to do, that each of these interpretations makes the conclusion of that argument irrelevant to its premises is not, I recognize, conclusive proof that Kant did not in fact argue that way. But it should be remembered that each of these alternatives is an *interpretation* of the text, not a claim about what Kant does or does not say. It is enough to show that such an interpretation is unacceptable if it can be shown to entail that the conclusion of the argument interpreted is irrelevant to the premises and, further, that another interpretation can be offered of the same argument which lacks such a defect. I have been trying to fulfill the first part of this task in the present section. I turn now to the second part of the task.

5

Concepts and Intuitions Again:
A Viable Interpretation

WE ARE LEFT with the fourth alternative: that intuitions are expressions for individuals and concepts are predicates in judgments. Kant's distinction would, on this view, hold between two kinds of expressions or representations which can appear in a judgment. All judgments about experience must contain two different kinds of representations. There is, first of all, the representation by which we signify the individual in experience; and there is, secondly, the representation by which we signify the predicate which is referred to the individual or individuals singled out by the subject expression.

But how does Kant's argument for the distinction between concepts and intuitions yield this as a conclusion? What Kant shows by the argument is, as I have already claimed, that intuitions cannot be reconstructed out of sets of concepts. If that conclusion is understood in the light of the fact that Kant himself groups both intuitions and concepts under the genus of representation, then what I have called the fourth alternative follows as a conclusion of that argument.[22] If intuitions cannot be built out of concepts, it follows that we cannot represent an intuition by means of a concept. Hence, any judgment which formulates a claim about experience must contain a representation which does not stand for a concept. Lacking such an expression, no such judgment can refer to experience at all. For all judgments of experience are judgments about empirical intuitions.

When I argue that the concept-intuition distinction is logical or semantical in character, I am not also arguing that the notion of an intuition plays only this role in Kant's philosophy. It quite clearly does not. An intuition is also the object to which any singular expression refers. But to show that an intuition also has this place is irrelevant to the present argument. Whatever other functions the notion of intuition has in the *Kritik,* it must at least have a semantical or logical function. For this is the conclusion that does follow from Kant's argument distinguishing concepts from intuitions.

But the evidence for the conclusion which I have attributed to Kant does not stand alone. There is independent evidence for the same conclusion. At B377 Kant contrasts an intuition with a concept, saying that they refer to an object in different ways. An intuition refers to an object directly, while a concept, Kant tells us, refers to an object indirectly by virtue of things that the object has in common with other objects.[23] The question arises: How could an intuition refer to an object if it were not itself a way of representing something as distinct from what is represented? It would be a mistake to answer

22. A320 = B376; cf. *Logik,* para. 1 (*Werke,* VIII, 88–89).
23. Cf. also A19 = B33 and A25 = B41.

this question by saying that an intuition represents an object directly in that it is a sign of other intuitions which can be presented. If an intuition is to do this, then it cannot do this just as an intuition. The only way in which an intuition can function as a sign of other intuitions is by being subsumed under a concept—which prevents an intuition from directly representing an object alone. But this is what Kant claims that an intuition can do. Such a claim implies that an intuition is a mode of signifying an object as distinct from the object signified.

Other evidence supporting the semantical interpretation of the concept-intuition distinction can be drawn from passages in which Kant characterizes all concepts as predicates of possible judgments. In one passage, for example, he says that "the only use which the intellect can make of concepts is to judge by means of them. . . . As predicates of possible judgments, concepts are referred to some representation of a not yet determined object." [24] If concepts are, one and all, predicates of possible judgments, then they cannot be the sole constituents of judgments about experience. In order to show this, let us consider a judgment that Kant would class as synthetic but which would consist of no representations save those for concepts. "This sugar is white" could serve as an example. If the subject expression, "This sugar," stood for a concept, then we could not distinguish (1) "This sugar is white" from the very different proposition (2) "Sugar is white." (1) and (2) are not equivalent because the truth of (2) is compatible with the falsity of (1). But if the expression in the subject place of the two propositions were a concept, then (1) and (2) would be logically equivalent. If the subject expression of (1) expressed a concept, then that expression could not denote the particular entity intended by the phrase, "this sugar." For the representation provided by a concept would be that which a number of things have in common; and, in that case, there would be no distinction between an expression about a particular sugary entity from one about sugar in general. This consequence follows, it should be noted, only from the assumption that

24. A68–69 = B93–94; cf. A25 = B40; A320 = B327; *Prolegomena*, para. 46 (*Werke*, IV, 86).

concepts can function as subject expressions in synthetic judgments. Once it is seen that there are representations which stand for particulars, then the embarrassing consequence which I have just sketched does not follow for Kant's theory of judgment. This is not, I acknowledge, conclusive evidence that Kant thought of intuitions as the subject expressions of synthetic judgments. But to attribute that view to Kant explains why he could have said that all concepts are *predicates* of possible judgments; and it saves Kant's view of judgment from a consequence otherwise fatal to it.

ᔆ6ᔆ

Intuitions and Kant's Break with the Tradition

THE INTERPRETATION of the concept-intuition distinction in the preceding section can explain the nature of Kant's break with the tradition over the issue of predication. How this break could have come about can be explained by first recalling one of the central doctrines of the *Kritik*, a good statement of which occurs at B749: "If we are to judge synthetically with a concept, we must go beyond the concept." This is the claim which caused the rift between Kant and his predecessors. While Kant's predecessors had recognized that some predicates could not be extracted from the subject concept of a judgment by human insight, they none the less retained the view that every predicate must be contained within the subject concept of a true proposition.

That there can be true synthetic propositions is a direct consequence of Kant's distintion between concepts and intuitions. The concept in a synthetic proposition, as we have seen, is a predicate. We must go outside the predicate in judging synthetically because we must link the predicate with an expression which stands for individuals. If Kant's arguments for the distinction between intuitions and concepts are sound, we can no more deduce the concept contained in a synthetic judgment from the subject expression than we can construct intuitions out of concepts. This is why Kant can say that we must go beyond the concept in a synthetic judgment. That such judgments can, contrary to the tradition before Kant, be true is a further consequence of the concept-intuition distinction. That there is such a distinction is proved by Kant's argument in the Aesthetic. And that the distinction is a logical one, I have argued, is a conclusion that genuinely follows from the argument Kant gives; hence, there must be true synthetic judgments.

The Kantian argument for the possibility of true synthetic propositions comes, then, to this. (1) Time and space are the conditions under which individuals are presented to us. (2) Time and space are pure intuitions. (3) Intuitions cannot be constructed out of combinations of concepts. (4) Representations referring to intuitions cannot contain conceptual representations as parts. Therefore, (5) Propositions referring to individuals presented in intuition are synthetic. Let us consider the grounds that Kant gives for each of the steps in this argument. The argument for (1) is familiar: We cannot, Kant says, think of objects without thinking of them in space and time; but we can think of space and time devoid of objects.[25] It follows that the individuals which are presented to us in our manifold must be spatial and temporal. The argument for (2) rests on a definition of pure intuition together with the citation of a fact about our manifold. The definition is that anything which is pure lacks any reference to the content of the manifold; since space and time are forms under which any particular object is given to us, it follows that space and time are pure intuitions. That (3) is the case follows from the argument which was given earlier in the present chapter. Step (4) is just the extension of (3) to cover parts of the proposition which refer to objects given in intuition. Step (5) is a direct consequence of all of these premises.

It should be noted that (5) cannot follow if the concept-intuition distinction is conceived as holding solely between the constituents of a judgment and what the judgment is about. On this view, the subject expression of a judgment would refer to intuitions; but if an intuition is merely the object of reference, then the only element in the

25. A24 = B39; A31 = B46.

judgment which can refer to it is a concept. That a concept can function in this way is not forbidden by the view that intuitions are sensations. To say that an intuition is a sensation leaves it entirely open whether these sensations are irreducible or can be constructed out of concepts. But this view has the disadvantage of being powerless to explain why there should be any synthetic judgments at all.

But Kant's argument shows more than that there are some synthetic judgments that are true. This would, as it stands, refute the traditional theory. But there is a stronger claim which follows from Kant's argument; the claim, namely, that the traditional theory is self-contradictory if applied to predication of individuals. This can be shown as follows: Leibniz held that true propositions about individuals are analytic and that the subject expressions of such propositions are individual notions. Such entities are, on Leibniz' theory, sets of concepts which collectively apply to one individual. But this puts the Leibnizian theory before a fatal dilemma. If individual notions are sets of concepts, then they cannot refer to individuals. And if such notions are not sets of concepts, then it cannot be the case that the predicate is contained in the subject expression of all true propositions.

Take the former alternative first. To say that such notions are sets of concepts makes them expressions which stand for what individuals share in common but not for individuals themselves. This is just a consequence of the view that concepts are predicates and that they stand for what individuals have in common. To construct expressions for individuals out of concepts is to succeed only in referring to what is common to many and hence not an individual. Sets of concepts are still expressions for what is common to many; hence, an analysis of individual expressions in terms of sets of concepts will no more yield expressions for individuals than an analysis in terms of one concept.

But what if individual notions are not sets of concepts? It would then follow that the predicate in judgments of which such a notion is the subject expression could not be contained in that notion. For if the predicate were so contained, then the subject expression would fail to represent the individual. In this way, then, to say that predicates are contained in the concept of the subject is incompatible with saying that the concept refers to an individual. This is the basis of the strong claim which follows from Kant's distinction between concepts and intuitions once it is understood as a semantical distinction.

We are now in a position to explain what Kant was opposing in the tradition before him and how, further, he could say that judgments of experience are one and all synthetic. What was primarily at issue between Kant and his predecessors was not whether we think one *concept* in another. That is, to be sure, one issue over which he disagreed with the tradition. But the major issue concerned whether the subject expressions of certain kinds of judgment contained the concepts which served as the predicates in such judgments. That they do not is the lesson of the concept-intuition distinction. And it is the reason why Kant could say that his distinction between synthetic and analytic judgments was novel. We can also explain how Kant could say that a judgment of experience must be synthetic. Such judgments are incapable of being analytic, not because an appeal to experience cannot certify a judgment to be analytic, but rather because no analytic judgment can refer to objects in experience.

All of this should arouse the suspicion that something is wrong with the way in which Kant describes his distinction between synthetic and analytic judgments. That description treats both judgments as relations of *concepts*. This has the defect, as I have been arguing, of distorting the character of Kant's break with the tradition; and, if pursued further, it will also have the defect of distorting the character of Kant's claim that there are synthetic *a priori* propositions. For if we take his *description* of the distinction between synthetic and analytic propositions as our guide, then a synthetic *a priori* proposition will be any whose predicate concept lies outside its subject concept and which none the less is universally and necessarily true. But if we look at the problem of the synthetic *a priori* through the concept-intuition distinction as it has been interpreted in this chapter, then synthetic *a priori* propositions take on a very different character: They are claims that objects, referred to by intuitions, fall under the predicates of such judgments. On the former interpretation, the problem of the synthetic *a priori* is whether we can combine two concepts independently of experience. On the latter interpretation, the problem is whether we can discover independently of experience that objects fall under a certain concept. What I have tried to do in this chapter is to show that the concept-intuition distinction is the basis of Kant's distinction between synthetic and analytic judgments. This is, however, only one piece of evidence for that conclusion. I shall now argue to the same conclusion from a consideration of how that distinction actually functions in the arguments of the *Kritik*.

CHAPTER THREE

Synthetic and

Analytic Judgments

W HEN KANT FORMULATES THE DISTINCTION between synthetic and analytic judgments, he tells us that they are different relations between *concepts*. In the first *Kritik*, for example, he distinguishes between a kind of judgment whose predicate concept is contained or thought within the subject concept from another kind of judgment whose predicate concept is not contained within the subject concept.[1] In the *Prolegomena* Kant gives a similar formulation of the distinction, saying:

If I say: all bodies are extended, I have not amplified my concept of body in the least, but only analyzed it. Extension, though not explicitly said of that concept, was already thought of it before the judgment. The judgment is thus analytic. On the other hand the proposition: some bodies are heavy contains

1. A6–10 = B10–14.

43

something in the predicate that is not really thought in the universal concept of body. It thus enlarges my knowledge in that it adds something to my concept, and hence must be called a synthetic judgment.[2]

The tradition of Kant scholarship has achieved an otherwise rare unanimity in holding that Kant's distinction turns on whether a given concept is part of another concept. There is, however, disagreement about the way in which Kant wanted us to discover what we think in a concept. At times Kant holds that we discover whether a proposition is analytic by the Law of Non-Contradiction.[3] We move from a proposition which is implicitly analytic to one that is explicitly analytic by substituting synonyms for synonyms. And it is clear that we can use this criterion without making reference, covert or otherwise, to what we think when we entertain a concept or to what is contained within a concept.[4] There are times, however, when Kant appears to use a different criterion. He tells us to take a concept apart and by simple inspection determine whether it contains another concept as a part.[5] To discover which of these criteria is dominant in Kant's thought about the synthetic-analytic distinction is not my purpose here. Whichever we take to be the dominant criterion, the distinction Kant appears to be making is a purely syntactical one, expressing only the relations of signs of the same logical type to one another. And these signs would all be what Kant calls *allgemeine Vorstellungen* or *Begriffe.*[6]

2. *Prolegomena*, para. 2 (*Werke*, VIII, 14 f.).

3. A random sample of the commentaries bears this point out: Norman Kemp Smith, *A Commentary to Kant's* Critique of Pure Reason (New York: Humanities Press, 1962), pp. 29 ff.; S. Körner, *Kant* (Baltimore: Penguin Books, 1964), pp. 18–19; H. J. Paton, *Kant's Metaphysic of Experience* (2 vols.; London: George Allen & Unwin, 1951), I, 82–87; Hans Vaihinger, *Kommentar zu Kants Kritik der reinen Vernunft* (2 vols.; 2d ed.; Stuttgart: Spemann Verlag, 1922), I, pp. 258 ff. These interpretations of the distinction are noteworthy, not for what they say, but for what they omit. They all explicate the distinction on the assumption that Kant used it as though it were a relation between concepts.

4. On this point see Lewis White Beck's article, "Can Kant's Synthetic Judgments Be Made Analytic?" *Kant-Studien*, XLVII (1955).

5. Cf. A718 = B746.

6. Cf. *Logik, Werke*, VIII, 399.

§ I §

Difficulties with Kant's Explicit Formulation of the Distinction

IT WOULD, however, be a serious mistake to think that this is what the distinction between synthetic and analytic judgments amounts to when Kant *uses* it. There are, in fact, two very different ways in which Kant understands the distinction. The first way of drawing the distinction (which I shall hereafter call the explicit or manifest theory) is the one I have just sketched. But, side by side with this way of drawing the distinction, there is a second view (which I shall hereafter call the implicit or hidden theory). This is a view which, as I hope to show, underlies some of the major arguments of the first *Kritik*. I shall argue to this conclusion by showing that there are at least four ways in which the explicit theory of the distinction conflicts with the way in which Kant acutally used the distinction in practice.

One such conflict arises when we compare the explicit formulation with Kant's claim that all mathematical judgments are synthetic.[7] Let us first consider the background of this claim. Kant held, first of all, that both mathematical and nonmathematical concepts are definable. And this is a view which he held from the time he wrote the essay *Ueber die Deutlichkeit der Grundsätze der natürlichen Theologie und der Moral,* where he was careful to distinguish the definition of a mathematical concept from that of a nonmathematical concept.[8] A mathematical concept is defined, on Kant's theory, by the construction of a concept in intuition. Defining concepts in other disciplines like, for instance, moral philosophy, consists in listing all of the constituents of those concepts. Kant also distinguishes between these two kinds of definition in terms of the way we arrive at them. In mathematics we *begin* by defining the concepts we use; in nonmathematical

---

7. The classical passages for this claim are A10 ff. = B14 ff. and *Prolegomena*, para. 2 (*Werke*, VIII, 14 f.).

8. *Werke*, II, 173 ff.

disciplines we reach the definition only as a conclusion of our inquiry.[9]

The merits of these distinctions as accounts of concept formation in mathematical and nonmathematical disciplines do not concern me here. All I am concerned to point out is that Kant says nothing to show that the *logical* structure of a definition differs when we move from mathematics to other disciplines. To argue, as he does, that we define a concept by constructing figures in space and reading off their properties may tell us something about the way geometers decide what constitutes a part of the concept they are considering. But it does not imply that a definition in mathematics is any less an analysis of a complex concept into its component parts than a definition, say, in moral philosophy. And that mathematicians arrive at the definitions they use in a way different from philosophers may be true; but it does not imply that the logical structure of a definition in mathematics must be different from that of a definition in philosophy.

If mathematical concepts are definable, then Kant has not shown why they cannot be complexes which are reducible to simpler parts. He may have seen important differences between definitions of mathematical and nonmathematical concepts. But nothing Kant says about such differences implies that the logical structure of definitions in one discipline is not just like that of definitions in every other discipline. Yet, if we compare his view of definition in mathematics with Kant's explicit formulation of the synthetic-analytic distinction, we may ask why all mathematical judgments are not analytic on Kant's theory. For the definability of mathematical concepts is at least prima facie evidence that the predicate concepts of mathematical judgments *are* thought or contained within the subject concepts of such judgments.

It is, however, a commonplace of Kant scholarship that Kant rejects an analysis of mathematical propositions that makes them out to be analytic. This, then, is the first conflict between Kant's explicit formulation of the synthetic-analytic distinction and the way in which he uses that definition in practice. Despite Kant's insistence on the important differences between definition of concepts in mathematics

9. *Ibid.*, pp. 176 ff. Cf. *Logik*, para. 101 (*Werke*, VIII, 444).

and in other disciplines, at no time does he use these differences as arguments against the view that a definition is anything but an analysis of a complex concept into its component parts. Yet, the definability of certain concepts is the very reason he gives for saying that many propositions are analytic. Why, then, does he hold this and still maintain that mathematical propositions are synthetic?

Kant's explicit formulation of the synthetic-analytic distinction cannot explain this. It cannot, that is, explain why Kant did not hold that all mathematical propositions are analytic. For nothing he says about the characteristics of a definition in mathematics is used to conclude that mathematical concepts are not definable. But, if Kant did not draw this conclusion, why did he persist in holding the position that mathematical judgments are one and all synthetic? This gap in Kant's argument should show us that the explicit account of his distinction between analytic and synthetic judgments cannot explain why he would call a very important class of judgments synthetic rather than analytic. And this points to the presence of another way of drawing the synthetic-analytic distinction which was implied by his arguments for the syntheticity of mathematical judgments but which is obscured by his reflective formulation of that distinction.

A second difficulty arises when we ask about the grounds on which we include one concept in another. On the theory of empirical concepts that Kant gives us at B756 and elsewhere in the first *Kritik*, the reason we have for including the concept of a property in that of a natural kind is that we find the referent of the one occurring constantly in conjunction with the referent of the other. Constant conjunction of properties is, in fact, the basis of empirical concept formation for Kant.[10] There is, however, a heavily populated class of synthetic judgments *a priori* whose subject and predicate concepts have referents that are constantly conjoined. But here, strangely enough, such a conjunction is not considered a sufficient reason for holding that the propositions in question are analytic. It should, however, be noted that I am not attributing the view to Kant accord-

10. Cf. *Logik*, para. 102 (*Werke*, VIII, 445); cf. also Lewis White Beck, "Kant's Theory of Definition," *Philosophical Review*, LXV (1956), 189 ff.

ing to which the assertion of a constant conjunction of properties is *equivalent* to the assertion of an analytic proposition. All I am claiming is that such a conjunction is regarded by Kant as a *reason* for adding certain concepts to our concepts of natural kinds. And I am asking why such a conjunction, though clearly present in the case of synthetic *a priori* judgments, does not give us a presumptive reason for thinking that the concepts of what we find constantly conjoined are analytically related to one another. Kant clearly does not think that a situation of the sort I have just described does give us a reason to make synthetic *a priori* judgments into judgments that are analytic. A good example of this line of argument is to be found in Kant's polemic against Eberhard. There Kant discusses the status of the proposition that substance endures through time, saying

> . . . Permanence is also an attribute of substance, for it is an absolutely necessary predicate of substance, but not contained in the concept of substance itself. Thus it cannot be extracted out of the concept by the Principle of Non-Contradiction through any analysis. And the proposition, "Every substance is permanent," is a synthetic proposition.[11]

What is puzzling about this passage is that the explicit formulation of the distinction between analytic and synthetic judgments cannot explain why the proposition discussed here should be synthetic rather than analytic. When a judgment is analytic on the theory of analyticity that Kant gives us, the referent of the predicate concept in such a judgment *must* be found constantly conjoined with the referent of the subject concept. That this is so is just another way of saying that one concept is contained in the other. But if this view of the evidence in terms of which a proposition is said to be analytic were applied without restriction, those very propositions which are counted as synthetic *a priori* would presumably be pronounced analytic. There is, then, yet another gap between the explicit formulation of the distinction and the way in which Kant uses it. For we are not told why the same reasons are used to count some judgments as synthetic and others as analytic. That we are not able to explain this by reference to

---

11. *Über eine Entdeckung, nach der alle neue Kritik der reinen Vernunft durch ältere entbehrlich gemacht werden soll*, in *Werke*, VI, 49.

the explicit formulation is an indication that there is another way of formulating the distinction which Kant assumes but does not state.

Thus we are left without an explanation of why the invariable conjunction of the referents of two concepts can be sufficient to make a proposition analytic in one context but synthetic *a priori* in another context. A similar problem occurs in another place in the *Kritik*. Sometimes Kant calls propositions involving the categories analytic, while at other times he calls such propositions synthetic. Two typical passages are these:

> If I leave out permanence (which is existence in all time), nothing remains in the concept of substance save only the logical representation of a subject—a representation which I endeavor to realize by representing to myself something which can exist only as subject and never as predicate.[12]

> For the same reason it follows that no synthetic proposition can be made from mere categories. For instance, we are not in a position to say that in all existence there is substance, that is, something which can exist only as subject and not as mere predicate.[13]

Each of these passages permits an inference which conflicts with the explicit theory of the synthetic-analytic distinction. In the first Kant describes a procedure of removing the concept of permanence from that of substance. But if permanence is part of the concept of substance, then it cannot be the case that the proposition, "Every substance is permanent," is synthetic. But Kant insists that such a proposition is synthetic.[14]

Consider the second passage. Kant claims that no synthetic proposition can be constructed out of categories. From this it follows that there are certain concepts which, although they are conjoined with the categories in judgments, cannot be part of the category. Kant says that mere categories will not enable us to say that there is substance in all existence. And the reason we cannot make synthetic propositions out of categories alone, Kant tells us, is that "so long as intuition is

12. A243 = B301.
13. A235 = B289.
14. Cf. footnote 11, above.

lacking, we do not know whether through the categories we are thinking an object." [15] But why should this be a reason for saying that there can be no synthetic propositions constructed from categories alone? If a synthetic proposition is a combination of concepts, then the syntheticity of that proposition is irrelevant to whether it has intuitions corresponding to any of the concepts in the proposition. Here, then, there is another discrepancy between Kant's arguments and his formulation of the synthetic-analytic distinction. We are told both that certain predicates are part of a concept and that they are not. And we are told that the relation a concept has to intuition determines whether it is included in another concept. The explicit theory of the synthetic-analytic distinction does not explain how it is possible that certain concepts can be part of other concepts and still not be thought within them or how the relation a concept has to intuition makes propositions in which it occurs synthetic.

There is another difficulty which lends support to the discrepancy which I have been pointing out. In his polemic against Eberhard, Kant argues that the Principle of Sufficient Reason cannot be deduced from the Law of Non-Contradiction. The reason he gives is that no amount of analysis can ever show that a synthetic proposition is analytic.[16] And we cannot, conversely, infer any synthetic claim from any set of analytic propositions. Both of these positions are argued repeatedly in the first *Kritik,* where Kant is concerned to distinguish between analysis of concepts from assertions that the concepts in question have something corresponding to them in experience.[17] Here I am not concerned with the cogency of any of the arguments Kant gives for making this distinction. All I want to point out is that they assume a theory of the synthetic-analytic distinction on which no synthetic proposition could ever be shown to be *covertly* analytic. If, let us suppose, it were possible to show that any proposition which had been thought to be synthetic was really only an analytic proposition in

15. A235 = B288.
16. *Über eine Entdeckung,* etc., in *Werke,* VI, 10.
17. Cf. B73 ff.; also A240 = B300.

disguise, then the distinction Kant makes between transcendental and formal logic—between establishing that concepts are not empty and establishing that concepts have certain kinds of connections with other concepts—would collapse. Now, Kant regarded his ability to make this distinction as one of his most significant advances over Leibniz' predicate-in-notion analysis of propositions.[18] One consequence of the Leibnizian analysis is that all true propositions are necessary. Thus, the Kantian distinction between synthetic and analytic propositions would, if we accept Leibniz' predicate-in-notion theory, turn out to be a distinction between implicitly and explicitly analytic propositions. And what is perhaps the most telling inadequacy of the explicit formulation of the synthetic-analytic distinction is that it cannot explain how Kant's new classification of propositions differs in the least from Leibniz'. Kant does, of course, emphasize that, no matter how we turn and twist the subject concept of a synthetic judgment, we will not be able to think the predicate concept in it. But why isn't this only a fact about our (relatively lamentable) analytic abilities as opposed

18. Cf. his essay on *Welches sind die wirklichen Fortschritte, die die Metaphysik seit Leibniz'ens und Wolff's Zeiten in Deutschland gemacht hat?* in *Werke*, VIII, 263 ff. There he argues that one of the significant advances in metaphysics lies in the distinction between the logical character of the Law of Contradiction and the Principle of the Identity of Indiscernibles. And he holds that this is achieved only through a prior distinction between analytic and synthetic judgments. Cf. also the discussion at B316–49, especially B325, and also *Über eine Entdeckung*, etc., pp. 47 ff. Some writers have denied that Kant was the first to make a viable distinction between synthetic and analytic judgments. The first to press this claim was, of course, Eberhard. A more recent representative of this view is A. O. Lovejoy, in his "Kant's Antithesis of Dogmatism and Criticism" (*Mind*, XV [1906], 191–214). Lovejoy holds that Wolff raised Kant's question about synthetic *a priori* propositions. For, according to Lovejoy, Wolff pointed out that "there are such things as *notiones foecundae*—'pregnant concepts'—whose peculiarity is that they contain *determinationes rei, per quas cetera quae in iisdem continentur, certa ratiocinandi lege colliguntur alia quae in iisdem non continentur*" (Lovejoy, p. 200). As I shall argue in greater detail later on, concepts, however pregnant, are still concepts and, as such, must have objects falling under them demonstrated or pointed out in intuition. And this is accomplished, not by giving honorific labels to concepts (as Wolff did), but by developing a theory of meaning to distinguish between pregnant and barren concepts.

to the logical structure of the proposition we are analyzing? Leibniz readily admitted that there are many propositions whose predicate concept cannot be seen *by us* to be contained in the subject concept.[19] But his conclusion from this was that the analyst of such propositions needed a God's-eye view of the subject concept.

This shows what is so suspicious about Kant's reflective statement of the synthetic-analytic distinction. The very reasons that Kant gives for holding that there is a distinction *in kind* between synthetic and analytic propositions (that we cannot think the predicate concept in the subject concept) were used by Leibniz to establish the distinction between explicitly and implicitly analytic propositions.[20] If we accept the explicit theory of the synthetic-analytic distinction, the consequence will be that Kant erected what he considered the most crucial distinction in his logical theory on the very grounds that Leibniz used for obliterating that distinction.

The conflicts I have been cataloguing thus far have consisted solely in the discrepancies that can be found between Kant's way of stating his theory and his way of applying it. I wish now to hold that even Kant's explicit formulations of the theory are not so straightforward as I indicated at the beginning of this chapter. Consider, for example, the passage in the first *Kritik* where he discusses the principle of all analytic judgments. He says this:

> The universal, though merely negative, condition of all our judgments in general, whatever be the content of our knowledge, and however it may relate to the object, is that they be not self-contradictory.[21]

---

19. C. I. Gerhardt, *Die philosophischen Schriften von G. W. Leibniz* (Berlin: Weidmann, 1875–90), IV, 432.

20. *Ibid.*, VII, 200: "The difference between necessary and contingent truths is indeed the same as that between commensurable and incommensurable numbers. For the reduction of commensurable numbers to a common measure is analogous to the demonstration of necessary truths; or their reduction to such as are identical. But as, in the case of such ratios, the reduction involves an infinite process, and yet approaches a common measure, so that a definite but unending series is obtained, so also contingent truths require an infinite analysis, which God alone can accomplish." Cf. also *ibid.*, V, 268.

21. A150 = B189.

He then goes on to contrast this with a characteristic that all synthetic judgments have:

> But in synthetic judgments I have to advance beyond the given concept, viewing as in relation with the concept something altogether different from what was thought in it. The relation is consequently never a relation either of identity or of contradiction.[22]

What is to be noted here is that Kant is particularly concerned to separate questions about the content (*Inhalt*) of a judgment from any consideration of whether that judgment is synthetic or analytic. On this formulation, what he is holding is that we can determine whether we have an analytic or a synthetic judgment by reflecting on the logical structure of the judgment. And, when we do this, we abstract from what the judgment asserts and the way in which it relates to an object.

But we must be careful here. For there appears to be evidence which runs counter to the interpretation I have just given of the passages above. At A154 = B193, for example, Kant says that "[t]he explanation of the possibility of synthetic judgments is a problem with which general logic has nothing to do. It not even so much as knows the problem by name." It is tempting to argue, on the basis of this passage, that the distinction between synthetic and analytic judgments is not a matter of formal logic for Kant.

But this is a temptation that must be resisted, at least on the evidence provided by A154 = B193. There are two reasons for this. First of all, what Kant says there is not that general logic knows nothing of the *distinction* between synthetic and analytic judgments but rather that general logic knows nothing of the problem of *justifying* synthetic claims. That general logic abstracts from the truth conditions of synthetic judgments does not imply the conclusion that general logic does not contain the concept of a synthetic judgment at all. And there is another reason why the passage under consideration is not able to support the claim that the synthetic-analytic distinction is unknown to formal logic as Kant conceives it. It should be noticed

22. A154 = B193.

that Kant considers the law of contradiction to be the universal condition of all our judgments in general. Thus we would be able to discover whether a judgment is self-contradictory and hence analytic by a tool of formal logic. But if this is so, then it follows that a tool of formal logic would enable us to discover whether a judgment is synthetic. The classification of judgments into analytic and synthetic is for Kant a conjointly exhaustive classification; hence, any nonsynthetic judgment would be *a fortiori* analytic and conversely. Thus formal logic must needs have a concept of syntheticity.

These passages should, however, be compared with the formulation Kant gives in paragraph 2 of the *Prolegomena*. There he says:

> But whatever origin judgments may have, or whatever they may be like as to their logical form, there is in them a distinction according to content, by virtue of which they are either merely *explicative* . . . or *ampliative*. . . . The former can be called *analytic* judgments, the latter *synthetic* judgments.

Here the distinction is not made according to the relations that concepts have to one another but rather according to what the judgment asserts or what it is about. When Kant puts the distinction this way, he appears to be holding that you cannot discover whether a judgment is synthetic or analytic until you have examined its content. And this cannot be examined as long as you are concerned with the relations of concepts to one another. What is significant about this way of stating the distinction is that it is a complete reversal of what Kant says in the *Kritik* at B189. There he was concerned to abstract from the content of judgments; here he wants to make the distinction by reference to the content of judgments.

One thing should be immediately clear: You cannot gloss over this glaring opposition between the two formulations by pointing out that the second is really a slip. The *Logik* contains a passage in which the theory is formulated just as it was in the *Prolegomena*. The passage is this:

> Extension (b) applies to every x to which the concept of body (a-b) applies—is an example of an analytic proposition.

Attraction (c) also applies to every x to which the concept of body (a-b) applies, is an example of a synthetic proposition.[23]

Consider what values the variable "x" can take. It surely cannot take words or concepts as values. Here Kant is talking about objects which fall under concepts, not the relation of one concept to another. Thus the distinction here is made, as it was in the *Prolegomena*, according to the relation of a concept to a class of objects. And this means that it is made in terms of the content of the judgment. For each kind of judgment is a different relation of a concept to a class of objects. Therefore, the view that Kant's variant descriptions can be explained in terms of a slip on Kant's part is hardly plausible. Both are present in his way of conceiving that distinction.

How is this divergence in the conception of the synthetic-analytic distinction relevant to Kant's explicit theory of that distinction? What it shows is that the explicit theory is incapable of accounting for passages in which Kant bases that distinction on the content of the judgment. When we consider the content of a judgment, what is being considered is the relation a concept has to an object. And what we want to know is whether there are any objects falling under a concept. If this is the basis of deciding whether a judgment is synthetic or analytic, then synthetic judgments cannot be constructed out of concepts alone. For we can determine whether one concept is contained in another by examining only part of the judgment. We do not have to attend to the relation of a concept to an object.

Thus the divergence in Kant's conception of the distinction outlines the presence of both an explicit and a hidden theory of judgment. According to the explicit theory, we can discover whether a judgment is synthetic by abstracting from its relation to an object and attending only to the relations of the concepts in the judgment. According to the hidden theory of judgment, we must consider the content of the judgment in making this discovery. We must, that is, attend to the relation of the concepts in the judgment to expressions which stand for objects. This is the reason that the divergence in Kant's formula-

23. *Logik, Werke*, VIII, 417.

tion of the synthetic-analytic distinction betokens a shift in the conception of that distinction.

⟨2⟩
Kant's Implicit Theory of Judgment

THE INADEQUACY of the explicit formulation of the synthetic-analytic distinction should by now be evident. It leaves inexplicable gaps in a number of the claims Kant makes; and, as I have just tried to show, it is by no means the formulation which Kant everywhere gives of that distinction. I shall now try to set out how Kant uses the distinction rather than how he describes it and discover why his description does not correspond to his use. The first step will be to show that Kant holds two different theories of judgment. Although he does express dissatisfaction with the theory of judgment which he inherits from Wolff, he never clearly tells us how he proposes to improve upon it.[24] Kant in fact wavers between the conception of judgment he gets from Wolff and another conception of judgment, which is presupposed by some of the most important arguments of the *Kritik*. This is a thesis which I shall seek to establish by showing that a second theory of judgment is implied by Kant's views on definition. Then I shall continue the argument, begun in Chapter Two, that Kant thought the distinction he made between intuitions and concepts demanded a new theory of judgment. In this way it will be possible to show that his divided opinions about the synthetic-analytic distinction are really consequences of his divided opinions about definition and judgment.

The only part of Kant's theory of definition which it is necessary to explore here is the distinction between a real and a nominal definition. Kant does not distinguish the two kinds of definition in terms of a definition of a word and a definition of a concept. The *definiendum* of each kind of definition is a concept, not a word. This is implicit in his

---

24. B141: "I have never been able to accept the interpretation which logicians give of judgment in general. It is, they declare, the representation of a relation between two concepts. . . . I need only point out that the definition does not determine in what the asserted *relation* consists."

general account of definition, when (at *Logik*, para. 99) he explains that a definition is "a sufficiently clear and distinct concept." The *definiens* of a nominal definition gives us what Kant calls the logical essence of an object, while a real definition explains "the possibility of the object out of inner marks." [25] The distinction he makes here is parallel to the one he made in the *Prize Essay* between making a concept clear (which he called the definition of a given concept) and making a clear concept (which he calls the exhibition of an object in intuition which falls under the concept). [26] Furthermore, this is supported by what Kant says at A218 = B265 of the *Kritik*, where he holds that we find the logical essence of anything by reflecting on the predicates constituting its definition. But, on Kant's view, this is to be strictly separated from giving the real definition of a concept, which is not done until we have succeeded in demonstrating the possibility of the referent of the concept. And this means, on the theory Kant is advancing, that we must find a correlate for the concept in pure or empirical intuition. [27]

The interest that the distinction between real and nominal definition has for us lies primarily in the startling conclusion that Kant draws from it. He begins, it will be remembered, with the fact that the procedure by which we find out what is contained in the concept of anything is different from that by which we find out whether the concept in question can be given a correlate in intuition. And he uses this fact to establish a distinction between two kinds of predicates that can enter into a definition. For him the predicates or notes (*Merkmale*) of a real definition are always synthetic, whereas the predicates

25. *Logik*, *Werke*, VIII, 447.
26. Cf. *Nachlass*, No. 2358: "Eine deutliche Erkenntnis machen: synthetische Merkmale Deutlichkeit. Oder Erkenntnis deutlich machen: analytische." Cf. also *Nachlass*, No. 2363: "Deutlichkeit durch analytische Merkmale, also *a priori* durch Begriffe von dem, was im Begriff liegt. Deutlichkeit durch synthetische durch das, was über den Begriff hinzukommt, also in der Anschauung als Merkmal gegeben ist (der reinen oder empirischen)." One of the earliest discussions of the difference discussed here is to be found in the *Untersuchung über die Deutlichkeit der Grundsätze der natürlichen Theologie und der Moral*, *Werke*, II, 176–79. Cf. also *Logik*, *Werke*, VIII, 444–45.
27. Cf. A218 = B265.

of a nominal definition are always analytic.[28] Thus, when a real definition of any concept is given, the predicates composing the *definiens*
are not contained within the concept being defined. Those predicates
which are not contained in the concept being defined are what Kant
calls determinations (*Bestimmungen*). Any predicate which is so contained is only a logical predicate.

There is an objection that can be made at once to this view of the
distinction between real and nominal definitions. I take it up here
because it will show that the distinction Kant is making here, despite
his misleading formulation, cannot be taken as a distinction between
two kinds of *predicates* but must be looked upon as a distinction
between a *predicate* and an *intuition*. The objection goes like this. The
distinction between making a concept clear and making a clear concept
would seem to be irrelevant to finding out whether any predicate is
contained in the concept being defined. For there are two things that
Kant appears to run together here. First: to make a clear concept
seems to have nothing to do with showing that objects can be given to
us which correspond to the concept we make. Second: even if we grant
for the sake of argument that we need something like a Kantian
theory of intuition to make a clear concept, we can still demand to
know what bearing this has on deciding what predicates we do or do
not think in the concept we have shown to possess a corresponding
intuition. This illustrates what is puzzling about Kant's distinction
between a logical predicate and a determination. If a determination is,
as Kant holds it is, really a kind of *concept*, then why can a determination not be thought within the concept whose *definiens* it in part
constitutes? As long as we take a determination to be a kind of
predicate, then, there is one decisive objection to Kant's way of
distinguishing nominal from real definitions. The distinction as Kant
states it rests on a confusion between deciding what we think in a
concept of anything when we conceive it correctly with the quite

---

28. A598 = B626: "Anything we please can be made to serve as a logical
predicate; the subject can even be predicated of itself; for logic abstracts from
all content. But a *determining* predicate is a predicate which is added to the
concept of the subject and enlarges it." Cf. *Nachlass*, No. 4055.

different question of finding out whether there is anything corresponding to that concept in experience.

This is, I hold, a decisive objection to Kant's theory as it stands. It assumes, of course, that Kant thinks of a determination as a concept and not as an intuition. But is there any evidence to suggest that a determination must be an intuition? It is true, of course, that Kant does not simply equate what he calls a determination with an intuition. All he says when he discusses the relation between the two is that we require a demonstration that a concept has a possible intuition corresponding to it if we are to know whether the concept in question is a determination or only a logical predicate. Still, it can be shown that only on the assumption that a determination is an intuition and not a concept will we be able to explain the most characteristic feature of a determination: that it can never be part of the subject of a judgment whose predicate it is.

Let us assume, then, that a determination is a concept and not an intuition. On this assumption there are two ways in which we could conceive of the relation between what Kant calls a logical predicate and a determination. We could take this relation to be that between a predicate variable and a specific value of that variable. A logical predicate would be the form of a concept in general (that it can be predicated of many), and a determination would be a specific kind of concept (". . . is red" or ". . . is a man") which would be a specific value of the first kind of concept. Some evidence for this reconstruction could be drawn from the distinction which Kant makes between the form and the matter of a concept.[29] On this distinction, we have specified the form of a concept when we say that it is universal and the matter when we have given the object it denotes. But this attempt at reconstruction would fail. For it cannot explain why the predicate which is the determination is not contained within the subject concept with which it is joined. It would not, that is, explain why a determination is a synthetic as opposed to an analytic predicate.

Rejecting this interpretation, we could attempt to understand the

29. *Logik, Werke*, VIII, 399.

distinction between a logical predicate and a determination as a function of what we know about the relation of a predicate to the world. A given concept will cease to be a logical predicate when we know that it can have something corresponding to it in intuition. Evidence for this interpretation could readily be found in something Kant says about the distinction between transcendental and formal logic. Now, whatever else he says about this distinction, Kant at least holds that we can draw the distinction in terms of what we know about concepts and propositions independently of their application to experience and what we know about these things after we have applied them to a domain of objects. Thus Kant holds that we can learn something when we examine the relations between concepts in a proposition; and he holds, further, that we may learn something quite different about these same concepts when we examine the relations they have to the objects they denote.[30] In the former case, we learn something about formal logic, while, in the latter case, we learn something about transcendental logic. Making reference to this distinction, we could argue that a concept ceases to be a logical predicate and becomes a determination of an object when we learn that it can have something corresponding to it in empirical or pure intuition. But this attempt at understanding the distinction between a logical predicate and a determination would fail just as the first did. For it is powerless to explain why the predicate about which we have this new information should cease to be a part of the subject concept of any proposition.

We have so far examined the consequences of the assumption that Kant understands a determination as a kind of concept. But neither of the ways of interpreting the relation between a logical predicate and a determination that are open to us on that assumption has succeeded in explaining the basis of that distinction. There is, however, another assumption which can explain the basis of the distinction. We can deny that a determination is a concept at all and claim that it is an intuition. In his theory of definition, Kant does not openly assert this. But it is only on this assumption that the distinction between logical

30. B79–83; cf. *Nachlass*, No. 2286.

predicates and determinations can be made intelligible. For we know from the arguments he presents subsequent to his essay *Vom Unterschiede der Gegenden im Raum* that intuitions cannot be reduced to concepts in the sense that they cannot be constructed out of any combination of concepts.[31] The argument from the Incongruity of Counterparts was used to show that we can have a concept of, say, a hand and still be unable to specify anything which we think in that concept by which we would distinguish between a left and a right hand. I am not concerned here with the cogency of this argument. The point that illuminates the distinction between a logical predicate and a determination is that a determination, like an intuition, cannot be thought within a concept.

Let us assess the importance of Kant's way of making the concept-intuition distinction for understanding the difference between a logical predicate and a determination. Kant characterizes a determination as a predicate about which we know that it has instances in experience. And it is this characteristic of a determination that prevents it from figuring as the predicate in an analytic judgment: We cannot discover by analysis of the subject concept that it contains a predicate instantiated in experience. Neither of these characteristics of a determination can be explained as long as it is regarded as a concept. To know that a concept is a determination is, of course, to know that it has instances. But this kind of knowledge is not derived from a concept, although it is knowledge involving a concept. The determination here is an intuition, information about which cannot be discovered by an analysis of any concept which it instantiates. Since an intuition cannot be constructed out of concepts, what we know when we know that a concept has instances in intuition is that it has objects falling under it. And this is what makes a determination an intuition. To say that a concept is a determination, if it is not to be rejected as simply false, must, then, be seen as an elliptical way of saying that a concept functions as a predicate in a true synthetic judgment. But such a

31. *Von dem ersten Grunde des Unterschiedes der Gegenden im Raum, Werke,* II, 393–400. Cf. *De Mundi sensibilis atque intelligibilis forma et principiis, Werke,* II, 412.

judgment cannot be composed of concepts alone. It must be a combination of concepts with intuitions. Accordingly, what Kant calls a real definition is a synthetic judgment.

Now, if a determination is to be understood as an intuition, we learn why Kant expresses such dissatisfaction in the first *Kritik* with the traditional account of a judgment as the relation between two *concepts*. He wants to hold that a characteristic feature of synthetic judgments is that they consist in the relation, not of two concepts, but of a concept and an intuition. And one significant piece of evidence for this interpretation is that his distinction between real and nominal definitions assumes the existence of certain kinds of entities which can figure as parts of a judgment without being thought within the concept which is the predicate in the judgment.[32]

That a synthetic judgment asserts a relation of a concept to an intuition is not, however, merely an assumption of Kant's theory of definition. He uses it in several of the most original arguments of the first *Kritik*. One such argument occurs in the Paralogisms, where he attacks a certain procedure of argument characteristic of rational psychology.[33] Kant was opposed to a procedure by which the rational psychologist tried to deduce a synthetic proposition from an analytic proposition. The analytic proposition with which rational psychology allegedly begins is that the ego is always a subject and never a predicate.[34] Kant is prepared to admit this proposition into the argument as explicative of the concept of "ego." But he objects to the

32. Independent evidence for this conclusion can be drawn from scattered references to judgment as a comparison of concepts with intuitions. He says, for example, in his essay *Welches sind die wirklichen Fortschritte*, etc., *Werke*, VIII, 253: "Damit eine Vorstellung Erkenntnis sei (ich verstehe aber hier immer ein theoretisches), dazu gehört Begriff und Anschauung von einem Gegenstande in derselben Vorstellung verbunden, so dass der erstere, so wie er die letztere unter sich enthält, vorgestellt wird." There is another passage in the *Kritik der Urteilskraft*, *Werke*, V, 261–62, where he says, "Wenn der Begriff von einem Gegenstande gegeben ist, so besteht das Geschäft der Urteilskraft im Gebrauche desselben zum Erkenntnis in der Darstellung (*exhibitio*), d.i. darin, dem Begriffe eine korrespondierende Anschauung zur Seite zu stellen." And in the first *Kritik* (as, for instance, at B93 ff.) Kant speaks of judgment as the application of concepts to intuitions.

33. A341 ff. = B399 ff.

34. A342 = B401.

inference drawn from this proposition that the ego is a substance. The inference is fallacious because it depends upon the equivalence of "subject" and "substance." And Kant denies that they are equivalent because substance, unlike subject, is defined in terms of a certain temporal sequence of intuitions.[35]

Given that "subject" and "substance" are not equivalent terms, the inference which Kant attacks is indeed fallacious. However, Kant claims, not merely that he has exposed an ambiguity in the rational psychologist's way of arguing, but that he has established something about the objective reality of the concepts used in that discipline. He gives his reasons for this when he says:

> That we are entirely right in resolving this famous argument into a paralogism will be clearly seen, if we call to mind what has been said in the General Note to the Systematic Representation of the Principles and in the Section on Noumena. For it has there been proved that the concept of a thing which can exist by itself as subject and never as mere predicate, carries with it no objective reality; in other words, that we cannot know whether there is any object to which the concept is applicable—as to the possibility of such a mode of existence we have no means of deciding—and that the concept therefore yields no knowledge whatsoever.[36]

The reason that "substance" is not equivalent to "subject" is that the former "demands for its proof data which are not to be met with in thought." [37] For "The concept of substance always relates to intuitions." [38] The concept of "subject" does not.

If we assume that Kant always understands judgment as involving a combination of concepts, then the relevance of these claims to his exposure of the formal fallacy in rational psychology will remain hopelessly obscure. We can grant that the predicate ". . . is a subject" is not the same kind of predicate as ". . . is a substance." But how does it follow from this concession that the propositions in which the former figures as a predicate are analytic, while the propositions

35. B408: "The concept of substance always relates to intuitions."
36. B412.
37. B407.
38. *Ibid.*

having the latter as a predicate are synthetic? To say that we can give examples of substances in intuition while no examples of subjects can be produced is not a relevant answer to this question. For the issue Kant has raised here is not about the reality of the class of things defined by either the concept of subject or substance. All he has said is that what is thought within the concept of substance is not what is thought within the concept of subject. On the assumption that *all* judgment involves a combination of concepts, the argument which Kant gives in the Paralogisms would seem to turn on the proper definition of the concept of the ego. And his dispute with the rational psychologist would turn on what we do or do not think in the concept of the ego, whereas Kant wants to make a point about what we can or cannot *experience*. Kant concedes the rational psychologist his definition; what Kant does not concede is that the rational psychologist has shown that there are any objects falling under his concept of the ego.

What was wrong with the rational psychologist's enterprise was not that he insisted upon adding a predicate to his concept of the ego that we do not think when we entertain the concept. If that were the issue between Kant and rational psychology, then Kant would only need to point out that his opponent's argument is a *non sequitur*. But this would not explain why the proposition that the ego is a substance is synthetic; and this in turn would leave unexplained why Kant is attacking rational psychology over what exists. The mistake of a rational psychologist was to think that a concept could perform the task of an intuition; the task, namely, of showing that the concept of the ego has objects falling under it which we can experience. What was objectionable about his procedure was not that he had failed to analyze the concepts he used with sufficient clarity. The rational psychologist failed of his purpose because he assumed that he could establish the existence of the ego as an object of possible experience by treating an intuition (the intuition of a certain kind of temporal sequence) as though it were a concept. Kant's point here, then, is that, in judging the ego to be a substance, the rational psychologist was applying the concept of "ego" to intuition. And this he had no right to do. For all his procedure permitted him to do was to *think* of the ego as a subject, which is a long way from showing that the referent of such a concept can be given in experience.

Now what does this argument show us about Kant's theory of judgment? Just this: Kant's argument here would have to imply that a synthetic judgment consisted in the claim that a concept had intuitions falling under it in order to make the point he intended to make against the rational psychologist. He is saying that you cannot show that a concept has an object falling under it by adding any kind of predicate to the concept of that object. The exegetical problem then becomes this. How does one move to the assertion of a synthetic judgment by asserting that the ego is a substance? Surely not by adding the *predicate* ". . . is a substance" to that of ". . . is a subject." For this makes it unintelligible how the resultant judgment —that the ego is a substance—should be one whit less analytic than the judgment that the ego is a subject. The only way in which we can explain how Kant could have thought that this judgment was synthetic rather than analytic is to assume that he thought of a synthetic judgment, not as the assertion of a relation between concepts, but rather as the claim that a concept (in this case, ". . . is a subject") had intuitions falling under it. On the assumption that a synthetic judgment asserted a relation between concepts, Kant's assertion that "The ego is substantial" is synthetic would have no support at all.

There is, then, a problem about the argument in the Paralogisms which the explicit theory of judgment is powerless to solve. There are two things about the argument which that criterion must explain if we are to look upon this part of the *Kritik* as something other than a curious ruin. First, what must be explained is the relevance of the synthetic-analytic distinction to the mistake which Kant imputes to rational psychology. Kant holds, it will be remembered, that the proposition, "The ego is substantial," does not follow from the proposition, "The ego is that which is subject of thought." And he also holds that the former does not follow from the latter because it, unlike the latter, is synthetic. But even if we assume that both of these propositions are analytic, one would not follow from the other just because the concept of "substance" is different from the concept of "subject." The second thing which must be explained here is why Kant should have believed that the concept of substance cannot be contained in the concept of an ego. That it cannot be so contained is one of the important parts of Kant's argument. But as long as we think of all judgment as involving the relation of concepts only, there appears to be no reason why any concept cannot be contained in any other concept with which it is compatible.

Kant's covert theory of judgment can solve both of the foregoing problems. It enables us to see the relevance of the synthetic-analytic distinction to the Paralogisms. The reason that the inference from the ego as subject to the ego as substance is fallacious is twofold: (1) Propositions in which the schematized category of substance figures as a predicate must be synthetic; and (2) No analytic proposition can entail a synthetic proposition. It is, of course, true that "substance" as it functions here is different from "subject." But they do not differ in their *conceptual* content. The *concept* of substance is just the concept of that which is subject but never predicate. Yet this does not exhaust our representation of substance. Kant reminds us of this when he points out that the concept of substance always relates to intuitions. Our representation of substance, then, unpacks into the conceptual representation of that which is subject but never predicate together with the representation of the intuitions which fall under it. And this explains why the proposition "The ego is substantial" must be synthetic. For it unpacks into the claim that the ego is subject of thinking and the claim that there are objects in intuition falling under the concept of a substantial ego. This latter component is what makes the proposition synthetic. For no proposition asserting that intuitions fall under a concept can be inferred from any purely conceptual relations that obtain between our thought of an ego and our thought of a subject of thinking. Thus the inference which Kant examines is fallacious because a synthetic proposition is being inferred from an analytic proposition. But this assumes that there are synthetic propositions which consist of a relation, not between concepts, but between concepts and intuitions.

The covert theory of judgment supplies us with the answer to the second difficulty that I mentioned above. Kant could have thought of the proposition "The ego is substantial" as synthetic because it consists in part of a proposition asserting that intuitions fall under the concept of a substantial ego. And this must be synthetic rather than analytic because, as Kant elsewhere argues, no representation of an intuition can contain representations which are conceptual.

The same lesson can be learned from yet another example of Kant's way of arguing. Let us compare Kant's discussion of what he calls the forms of judgment with the particular system of synthetic *a priori* judgments which arise from the application of the forms of judgment to experience.[39] Owing to the extreme complexity of these sections of the first *Kritik*, I shall restrict my point here to the properties of judgment Kant discusses under the heading of "relation" and, more particularly, to the subject-predicate relation.[40] What I am going to say about this part of Kant's Table of Judgments can be easily extended to cover all the other parts of the table. Here I want to explain why the subject-predicate relation should yield a synthetic rather than an analytic judgment when it is put in the context of transcendental logic. And I want to argue that this move in Kant's argument will remain opaque unless we take him to be assuming the theory of synthetic judgment that I have already mentioned.

When Kant introduces the Table of the Forms of Judgment, he describes what he is doing by saying that he is enumerating the functions of thought in general.[41] He does not say that these functions of judgment are themselves judgments. All he claims here is that they are properties or moments that belong to every judgment. One of the properties that every categorical judgment has is that it is a relation of a subject to a predicate. When Kant applies this relation to a domain of objects, what was the *form* of judgment in general yields a particular judgment which Kant holds to be synthetic. Thus when we apply the form of judgment called the subject-predicate relation to experience, we must, as Kant says, ". . . advance beyond the given

39. A73–76 = B98–101; A148 = B188; and esp. A160 = B200.
40. A72–74 = B98–99.
41. A68 = B93.

concept, viewing as in relation with the concept something altogether different from what was thought in it." [42] To make this comparison ". . . a third thing is necessary in which alone the synthesis of two concepts can arise." [43]

The transition in Kant's argument from the Forms of Judgment to an application of these forms to the domain of objects given to us in intuition can be illustrated by taking the example of the concept of substance and comparing its place in both parts of the argument. The concept of substance appears in Kant's discussion of the Forms of Judgment as "a something which can be thought only as subject, never as a predicate of something else." [44] This states a relation of thought in a judgment; hence it is a concept of formal logic. And the proposition that substance is something that can be thought only as subject and never as predicate of something else is analytic. But when this relation of elements in a judgment is applied to a manifold of intuition, the predicates which we apply to it—in particular, permanence through time—are not thought within the concept of substance but are added to it. This, then, is the transition which must be accounted for by the distinction between synthetic and analytic judgments.

This move of Kant's is inexplicable on the assumption that a synthetic judgment is just a combination of two concepts. For we may ask how information that a form of judgment applies to a manifold of intuition renders the judgment that substance is permanent through time synthetic so that the predicate concept is not thought within the subject concept. Why does the fact that I apply a relation of concepts to a domain of objects have anything at all to do with whether I think one concept in another when I make the application? So far from the application of the forms of judgment to experience being able to give us a system of synthetic *a priori* propositions, it can give us no reason why the propositions in question might not just as well be analytic. The reasons given by Kant for the fact that a system of synthetic *a*

42. A154 = B193.
43. A154 = B194.
44. A146 = B186.

priori propositions springs from the application of the Table of Judgments to experience are quite compatible with the analyticity of those propositions. And pointing this out amounts to a rejection of those reasons.

But there is another explanation that is open to us. We can say that Kant is using a different theory of synthetic judgment from the one he says he is using. The theory that is implicit in his movement from the Table of Judgments to the Analytic of Principles is that a judgment is synthetic when it asserts, not that one concept is outside the scope of another, but that a concept has an intuition corresponding to it. Thus when Kant argues that the predicate, ". . . is permanent through time," is synthetically related to substance, what he can be taken to argue is that the relation holds, not between the predicate and the *concept* of substance, but rather between the predicate, which is a concept, and substances which fall under that concept. The transition from the Forms of Judgment to their application to intuition is, accordingly, a move from defining the categories to relating them to objects which fall under them. The concept of substance will be related to intuition in the judgment that substance is permanent through time. To say that substance is permanent in time is, in this context, to assert that the concept of substance has objects falling under it. And these objects are intuitions. Only on this assumption can we explain how the Forms of Judgment can yield synthetic judgments when they are applied to experience, the application consisting in the assertion that the concepts appearing in that Table have intuitions falling under them.

ᘓ 3 ᘔ

Kant's Implicit Theory Again:
The Evidence Reconsidered

LET US SUMMARIZE the kinds of evidence on which I claim that there are two theories of judgment in the first *Kritik* and, consequently, two theories of the synthetic-analytic distinction. The evidence falls into two classes, the first of which consists of discrepancies in some of Kant's arguments between what he claims and the reason why he would make such claims. Thus he says that all mathematical judgments are synthetic *a priori*. But an examination of his theory of definition in mathematics shows that there is no reason why mathematical propositions should be synthetic at all. Another such discrepancy occurs in the grounds on which Kant distinguishes between analytic and synthetic *a priori* propositions: the invariable conjunction of certain clusters of properties is enough to justify including them as part of the definition of an empirical concept. Yet synthetic *a priori* propositions describe a universal and necessary conjunction; but that is not, for Kant, a reason to pronounce such propositions analytic. A third discrepancy occurs within the context of *a priori* concepts: There are some concepts which can never be parts of other concepts with which they are conjoined. And the characteristic in virtue of which one concept can combine only synthetically with another is that the concept in question refers to intuitions. And this conflicts with the description of a synthetic judgment: that a concept has intuitions corresponding to it does tell us something about the concept; but it does not tell us whether that concept is contained in another. And finally there is a discrepancy between Kant's claims about the synthetic-analytic distinction and his relation to his predecessors. There is no reason why the distinction which Kant marks between synthetic and analytic judgments is not the same distinction as that which Leibniz marks between explicitly and implicitly analytic propositions. All of these difficulties show that the description given of the synthetic-analytic distinction in the *Kritik* cannot explain why Kant argues as he does.

But there is also a kind of evidence which shows, not that there are discrepancies in Kant's arguments, but rather that his arguments actually assume a different theory of judgment than the one Kant frequently tells us he is holding. There are three main arguments in this class. The distinction between nominal and real definition presupposes the view that what Kant calls a determination is an intuition; and this in turn presupposes that real definitions are synthetic *a priori* judgments which are relations between intuitions and concepts, not merely between two concepts. And the argument in the Paralogisms makes a similar assumption. Unless we take a synthetic judgment to be a relation between an intuition, which is the subject of the judgment, and a concept, which functions as the predicate in the judgment, we cannot explain how Kant could have criticized the rational psychologist for trying to infer a synthetic from an analytic proposition. The third argument assuming a different theory of judgment is in the transition from formal to transcendental logic. The judgments formed from concepts in the former are, Kant says, analytic; when these concepts are applied to intuition, the judgments formed out of them are synthetic.[45] And the only way of explaining this is to say that synthetic judgments contain intuitions as their subject expressions.

We are now in a position to give a general characterization of the theory of judgment which, as I have been arguing, Kant assumes but does not formulate. I shall begin by examining a passage in the *Kritik* where Kant discusses the relation of a synthetic judgment to the world. There Kant tells us the following:

Judgment is therefore the mediate knowledge of an object, that is, the representation of a representation of it. In every judgment there is a concept which holds of many representations, and among them of a given representation that is immediately related to an object. Thus in the judgment, "all bodies are divisible," the concept of the divisible applies to various other concepts, but is here applied in particular to the concept of body, and this concept again to certain appearances that present themselves to us.[46]

45. When I say that judgments formed from concepts in the Table of Judgments are analytic, this must be distinguished from the different (and false) claim that the concepts in that table apply only to analytic judgments. These concepts function in two ways. They classify logical relations in all judgments, both synthetic and analytic. And they also figure as parts of some judgments. This second function is the one under discussion here.

46. A68 = B93; also A19 = B33; A25 = B41. Cf. *Die falsche Spitzfindigkeit der vier syllogistischen Figuren*, para. 1 (*Werke*, II): "Etwas als ein Merkmal mit einem Dinge vergleichen heisst *urteilen*. Das Ding selber ist Subjekt, das Merkmal das Prädikat. Die Vergleichung wird durch das Verbindungszeichen *ist* oder *sind* ausgedrückt, welches, wenn es schlechthin gebraucht wird, das Prädikat als ein Merkmal des Subjekts bezeichnet, ist es aber mit dem Zeichen der Verneinung behaftet, das Prädikat als ein dem Subjekt entgegengesetztes Merkmal zu erkennen gibt." Cf. esp. *Nachlass*, No. 4684:

A judgment consists of two parts. There is, first of all, the relating of one concept to another. Thus when I judge that all bodies are divisible, I am relating the concept of divisibility to the concept of body. But this is only one part of the judgment. I then relate both concepts to what Kant describes as "certain appearances that present themselves to us." But, if this is what Kant understands by a judgment, then every synthetic judgment will include intuitions. For an intuition is the element in the judgment which is immediately related to an object.

The hidden theory, then, is as follows. There is the *act* of judging, which is found in my relating one concept to another and then both of them to intuitions. There is, secondly, the *content* of this act, which, in this case, would be two concepts and the intuitions to which they are related. And there is, finally, the verbal expression of this content, in which there would be an expression for each element in the content of the judgment. This formulation fits the schematic representation of a judgment, quoted earlier in this chapter, which Kant gives us in the *Logik*.[47] The variable "x" which precedes the variables for concepts would take as its values expressions for intuitions.

But what distinguishes this theory of judgment from the one that Kant explicitly holds? The main difference lies in the relation of intuition to judgment. On what I have called the explicit theory, intuition is what the content of a synthetic judgment refers to. An intuition is the fact to which we make reference in ascertaining whether the referents of the concepts composing the judgment are combined in the way in which the judgment asserts them to be combined. The official formulation of the synthetic-analytic distinction assumes that intuitions are only objects to which concepts refer. An intuition cannot, on this view, be a part of a judgment. The theory of judgment which is not represented in Kant's official formulation of

---

"In analytischen Urtheilen geht das praedicat eigentlich auf den Begriff a, in synthetischen auf [die Bedingung des] das object des Begriffes, weil das praedicat im Begriffe nicht enthalten ist." Cf. also Kant's letter to Reinhold (1789), in *Werke*, IX, 402.

47. *Logik, Werke*, VIII, 417.

the synthetic-analytic distinction is the direct consequence of the logical interpretation of the concept-intuition distinction. An intuition is not only an object which can fall under concepts. It is, on this theory, a part of the judgment itself. And it is not hard to see why this view of what an intuition is would demand a view of judgment that diverges greatly from the official doctrine. To judge of objects demands that there be a representation in the judgment in virtue of which we can relate a concept to an object. And, as I have argued in Chapter Two, no concept can relate in this way to an object. What is demanded as a condition of referring to any object is a way of representing an object as a particular. And this is what requires a revision of the conception of judgment.

The official doctrine of the synthetic-analytic distinction had turned on the inclusion or exclusion of concepts. This distinction is preserved in the theory of judgment which is concealed in the arguments of the *Kritik*. On this theory, a synthetic judgment will be such that its parts are not included one in the other. But this will be the case, not because one of the concepts composing such a judgment is not included in another. It will rather be the result of the argument, presented in the Aesthetic, that no expression referring to an intuition can yield any expressions referring to concepts. Similarly, the official theory of the synthetic-analytic distinction requires that, in an analytic judgment, the predicate be included in the subject concept. And this requirement is preserved by the unofficial theory. The subject expression of such judgments stands for a concept. And since the truth of such judgments cannot be ascertained by looking at intuitions (otherwise the judgment would be transformed into a quite different judgment asserting that a concept has intuitions falling under it), the only other way in which such a judgment could be certified as true is by the relations of one of its constituents to another. And this is where the criterion of inclusion is preserved.

The reason that this new theory of judgment is obscured in the *Kritik* is to be found in a clash of two very different ideas. The first is the idea that a judgment must consist in a relation between two concepts. Although Kant was dissatisfied with the account which the tradition tendered of the character of this relation, he did not reject the account of the representations composing a judgment. They must both be concepts. Thus when he says that a judgment is the representation of a representation of an object, it is clear from the examples he gives that concepts are the only representations admitted. But this first idea clashes with the revolutionary import of the concept-intuition distinction: that no concept can stand in an immediate relation to an object. For this entails that there must be a kind of synthetic judgment which contains a singular representation in the subject place of the judgment. And thus two ideas clashed. The upshot of this clash was that the new insight about singular representations was accommodated to the traditional theory of judgment: The intuition was treated only as the referent of the concepts in the judgment.

⟨€4€⟩
The Place of the Implicit Theory in the Kritik

I BEGAN THE PRESENT CHAPTER by cataloguing four discrepancies in Kant's argument. I attributed them to the misleading character of the official theory of the synthetic-analytic distinction. And my purpose here is to show how the implicit theory of judgment which I have been attributing to Kant can remove these discrepancies. This will supply independent evidence of the presence of that second theory in the *Kritik*. And it will enable us to see transitions in arguments where there would be gaps.

1. The first discrepancy arose between the place of definition in mathematics and the reason for thinking that mathematical judgments are synthetic. Nothing Kant says about definition in mathematics constitutes a reason for thinking that the concepts in mathematical propositions might not be defined in just the way concepts in other disciplines are and thereby be analytic. Thus, given adequate definitions of number and the logical operation of addition, there is no reason for Kant to say that arithmetical propositions are synthetic.

And that this is a possibility is not excluded by anything he says regarding the function of a definition in mathematics.

Here I shall consider only the arithmetical proposition, $7 + 5 = 12$, which Kant cites as a paradigm case of a synthetic proposition. Kant says this about the example:

> The concept of 12 is by no means already thought in merely thinking this union of 7 and 5; and I may analyse my concept of such a possible sum as long as I please, still I shall never find the 12 in it. We have to go outside these concepts, and call in the aid of the intuition which corresponds to one of them . . . adding to the concept of 7, unit by unit, the five given in intuition.[48]

If the proposition, $7 + 5 = 12$, is taken to be a combination of concepts, then it can be shown to be analytic, given adequate definitions of the concepts involved, together with a definition of the operation of addition. And nothing Kant says about the character of definition in mathematics would close this possibility. How, then, could he have said that "it is then obvious that, however we might turn and twist our concepts, we could never, by the mere analysis of them, and without the aid of intuition, discover what [the number is that] is the sum"?[49]

I do not propose to defend Kant's theory of arithmetic, for I believe that his reason for thinking arithmetical propositions synthetic is mistaken. Thus he is right in pointing out that "12" is a different concept from "7," "5," or the concept of their sum. But the proposition under discussion here can be shown to be analytic if it is shown that it follows from analytic propositions. All I wish to do is to show why Kant could have excluded the possibility of showing such propositions to be analytic. He must have reasoned as follows. Each of the concepts in arithmetical propositions is different from the others; hence, to give the definition of one concept is not to discover the definition of any of the other concepts in it. The reason for this is that the definition of the concept "7" or the concept "5" will consist of

48. B15.
49. B16.

conceptual marks or notes which will only serve to distinguish one of these numbers from the other. Either of these numbers could, of course, be "defined" by enumerating the units which fall under the concept being defined. This would not, for Kant, be a relation between concepts but rather a relation between a concept and objects which fall under it. And so, given Kant's premise that such a definition would state a relation between a concept and the objects falling under it, no arithmetical proposition could be analytic because every such proposition would relate a collection of objects to a set of concepts. That $7 + 5 = 12$ is, accordingly, a claim that the sum of the groups delimited by 7 and 5 is a group of twelve: such a claim would be that the number of objects falling under 7 and 5 is 12. To discover this sum, then, it would not be enough to analyze the concept of "7" or "5." For these are different concepts; and the analysis of them would not reveal that the sum of a collection of seven and five is twelve.

This makes it intelligible why Kant excludes the possibility of making arithmetical propositions analytic by the introduction of definitions. It is the result of the way in which he interprets the claim that $7 + 5 = 12$. He looks upon it as a claim about objects. And no such claim can be verified by the analysis of concepts. Hence Kant can admit the possibility of a definition of all the concepts involved in arithmetical propositions and still maintain that such propositions must be synthetic. But this assumes that there are judgments which involve a relation of a concept to an intuition—which is precisely the implicit theory of synthetic judgment. The reasoning comes, then, to this. The concepts of numbers are concepts of collections of objects. But objects cannot be deduced from concepts or constructed out of concepts. Propositions stating relations between numbers are therefore propositions which relate concepts to objects. This makes them synthetic.

2. The second discrepancy to be explained is this. In the theory of empirical concept formation, Kant holds that constant conjunction of properties in experience is a reason for inclusion of the concept of one

of these properties in the concept of the other. But the referents of the concepts in metaphysical synthetic *a priori* propositions are also constantly conjoined. And this is not a reason for including the concept of the one in the concept of the other.

But why is this distinction not merely arbitrary? If all propositions were relations of concepts, then it would be quite arbitrary. But what distinguishes the cases is that, in the case of empirical concepts, Kant is talking about the reasons we have for including one concept in another. What he is talking about in the case of propositions that are synthetic is whether objects fall under concepts. Thus it is true that the referents of the concepts involved in metaphysical synthetic *a priori* propositions are universally and necessarily conjoined. This is not a reason for making such propositions analytic because what they assert is that it is universally and necessarily the case that objects fall under the predicate concept. And to assert that such is the case is different from asserting that properties are constantly conjoined. Hence to say that certain features of experience are constantly conjoined means something very different in the context of empirical concepts from what it means in the case of pure concepts. In the former context the claim concerns our reason for constructing an empirical concept in one way rather than another. In the latter context the claim concerns the relation of a concept we have already constructed to the objects which fall under that concept. The distinction Kant makes, therefore, is not arbitrary.

3. But there is another discrepancy. Why should Kant make the relation which a concept has to intuition a reason for holding that the concept either can or cannot be thought within another concept? This discrepancy is prominent in Kant's discussion of propositions containing categories.

This move is explicable once it is remembered that, on the implicit theory, there are synthetic propositions which relate concepts to singular representations, which are intuitions. Thus to show that a concept is related to intuition is to assert a synthetic proposition. And this is what is involved in Kant's discussion of categories. When they lack any relation to intuition, they cannot be parts of synthetic judgments.[50] And it is only by relating them to intuition that synthetic judgments arise. But this can be explained only on the assumption that there are synthetic judgments which contain singular representations as one of their constituents. If this were not the case, then Kant's remark that the categories cannot form synthetic judgments apart from intuition would simply be false.

4. There is, finally, the difficulty which turned on understanding just how Kant's distinction between synthetic and analytic propositions marks an advance over the Leibnizian distinction between contingent and necessary truths. The primary difficulty here was to see how Kant could hold that a synthetic proposition could not be transformed into an analytic proposition. On the Leibnizian theory, *all* true synthetic propositions were implicitly analytic propositions. This is a conclusion that Kant denied; and, as long as we accept the usual view of his theory of judgment, we will have to say that he failed conspicuously in making good his denial.[51] What distinguishes his theory from Leibniz' is that Kant introduced reference to an object located in space

50. A235 = B289.

51. Kant appears, at one point, to hold a view of the synthetic-analytic distinction that is Leibnizian. In *Nachlass*, No. 3928, he says: "Wenn man den ganzen Begriff hätte, wovon die notionen des subjekts und praedicats *compartes* seien, so würden die synthetischen Urtheile sich in analytische verwandeln. Es frägt sich, wie weit hier willkürliches sei." This should not, however, be viewed as an exception to the view that I have attributed to Kant. When he wrote this, he had not yet developed the position according to which intuitions are to be distinguished from concepts. Thus, when he wrote this passage, he could not yet have made the distinction between synthetic and analytic judgments one of kind. Evidence for this reading of *Nachlass*, No. 3928, can be drawn from what Kant says in a passage written shortly before the present one. In *Nachlass*, No. 3920, he says this: "Wenn irgend etwas x, welches durch eine Vorstellung erkannt wird, mit einem andern Begriffe b verglichen wird, entweder dass es diesen einschliesse oder ausschliesse, so ist dieses Verhältnis im Urtheil. Dieses Urtheil ist also entweder die Erkenntnis der Einstimmung oder Widerstreits, so dass in dem [Begriffe von] dem Dinge x, welches ich durch den Begriff a kenne, entweder b als ein Theilbegriff enthalten ist, oder also x [auch], welches durch a erkannt wird, auch durch b erkannt werden kann, oder dass durch x den Begriff von b aufhebt." What is important here is that he thinks of values of the variable "x" as concepts, not intuitions. Thus a synthetic judgment is still bound to be the assertion of a relation between concepts.

and time as part of the judgment. The issue then turns on whether the content of the judgment referring to objects in space and time can be merely a relation of concepts. Kant denied that it could when he denied that space and time are concepts. This denial, as I argued earlier, implies the view that there are some judgments whose content consists in the relation of a concept to an intuition and not merely in a relation between concepts. If there are judgments of this kind, it follows that they cannot be reduced to analytic judgments. For no intuition can ever be part of a concept. And a synthetic judgment, which asserts that a concept has a corresponding intuition, is not merely an analytic judgment awaiting an infinite analysis. No amount of analysis could ever tell us that the concept had such an intuition corresponding to it. Consequently, the second theory of judgment which I attributed to Kant enables us, as the first did not, to explain how he could have thought his distinction between synthetic and analytic judgments marked a major departure from the Leibnizian tradition.

I have yet to explain how my interpretation of Kant's theory of judgment can remove the apparent incoherence in his formulation of the synthetic-analytic distinction. In some passages he tells us that the distinction is drawn on the basis of the content of judgments; in others, that it holds independently of the content of the judgment. This difficulty disappears once it is seen that he is presupposing two different theories of judgment. If, for example, we consider only the theory according to which all judgment is the relation of concepts, then the distinction will be independent of what the judgment is about, i.e., the objects which are referred to by the judgment. But if we consider the theory of judgment according to which it is a relation of concepts to objects, then to say that a judgment is synthetic will be to tell us something about the content of the judgment. Kant moves from one conception of judgment to the other; and he conceives of the synthetic-analytic distinction differently in each case.

Someone accustomed to reading the *Kritik* in terms of Kant's explicit theory of judgment will, perhaps, still have a lingering reservation about the position I have been arguing. And this reservation is, no doubt, produced by an ingrained conviction that intuitions cannot function as logical entities at all. For, so it will be said, intuitions must be able to function as that to which synthetic judgments refer and that by reference to which the concepts in the judgment are combined. But if intuitions are parts of judgments, they cannot do this—from which it allegedly follows that there would be nothing existing outside the synthetic judgment to justify the combination of concepts composing the judgment.

The only way known to me of removing this kind of reservation is to point out that I am not denying that intuitions are objects which exist apart from judgments. What I am denying is that the class of intuitions is exhausted by the enumeration of all extrajudgmental objects. And this is only another way of saying that "intuition" has a use in Kant's idiom other than the designation of extrajudgmental objects. Thus there are intuitions which justify the synthesis of elements in synthetic judgments. But the elements in such judgments— and this is the position I have been at pains to argue—cannot be made up entirely of concepts.

⚙5⚙
The Implicit Theory and Ontology

THE NEW THEORY of judgment in the *Kritik* implies a new theory of metaphysical judgments. If you follow the explicit theory, a metaphysical judgment, if is it synthetic, will consist of two pure concepts and will make a claim that no possible experience can verify or falsify. The problem which judgments of this kind raise for Kant is how we are to know that what they claim is true. But there is a second way of looking at metaphysical judgments which is the result of applying the implicit theory of judgment to such judgments. A metaphysical judgment will consist of a pure concept functioning as the predicate and an expression for individuals functioning as the subject expression of the judgment. Thus all metaphysical judgments will be claims that objects fall under pure concepts.

But there are several problems attached to the new theory of what a metaphysical judgment is. The first problem concerns the analysis of the pure concepts which figure as predicates of such judgments. Kant tells us that a pure concept contains no element referring to intuition.[52] But if the predicates of metaphysical judgments are pure concepts, then how can any objects fall under them which are encountered in the manifold of our intuition? A metaphysical judgment is, on the theory implicit in the *Kritik,* a claim that objects fall under pure concepts. But if these concepts contain no element to distinguish their application to the manifold of our sensibility from any other manifold, it follows that there are no objects in our manifold which fall under these concepts.

This is closely associated with the second problem about metaphysical judgments. If there are metaphysical judgments which contain expressions referring to individuals, what are the individuals to which such expressions refer? Any object that one singles out in our manifold as falling under a pure concept will not be the referent of the subject expression of the metaphysical judgment because there must be some element in the predicate of that judgment in virtue of which the object can fall under it. But if no pure concept contains an element which distinguishes its reference to our sensibility from its reference to any other, then how can it be predicated of any object which is given to us in our sensibility? To predicate a concept of any object is to claim that it has a property in virtue of which it falls under the concept in question. If the concept lacks a property which is instantiated in our manifold, then it cannot be true that any object in our manifold falls under it. And it will do no good to argue here that, if a concept like a pure category is instantiated in every manifold, it will be *a fortiori* instantiated in ours. To say of a pure category that it is *compatible* with any manifold is not to say that it is *instantiated* in any manifold. And so the problem remains. A pure category must have an element in it which is exemplified in our manifold. But the element in our manifold which exemplifies it must be different from the element

52. Cf. *Prolegomena,* para. 1 (*Werke,* VIII, 13).

in any other manifold which would exemplify the pure category which can be exhibited in our sensibility.

These two problems about metaphysical judgments stand together. To locate the objects in our manifold that fall under the pure categories is to locate the element which must have a corresponding element in the category. And to locate such an element is to discover the objects to which the subject expressions of metaphysical judgments refer. In the following chapter I shall argue that transcendental schemata are such objects, that they must fall under categories, and that the categories must contain concepts of these transcendental schemata. This will prepare the ground for the argument, which I shall present in Chapter Five, that the metaphysical propositions which Kant tries to demonstrate must be understood in the light of his implicit theory of judgment.

CHAPTER FOUR

Intuitions and

Schemata

O<small>UR DISCUSSION OF</small> K<small>ANT'S</small> <small>HIDDEN THEORY</small> of syntheticity sets us a problem. We must discover how Kant distinguishes between kinds of pure intuition and how he explicates the relation of correspondence between a pure concept and a pure intuition. Both of these tasks are necessary if we are to understand how Kant conceives of a synthetic *a priori* judgment. Yet the outcome of the last chapter makes it difficult to accomplish either of these tasks. If Kant did profess one theory of syntheticity and use another, then we cannot expect that his exposition of the nature of synthetic *a priori* judgments will accord with his hidden theory of syntheticity. We cannot, therefore, look to his professed criterion for light about *a priori* judgments that are synthetic according to his hidden theory. In the face of this difficulty I shall pursue the following course. On his explicit theory of syntheticity, Kant did think that the subject and predicate concepts of a synthetic judgment *a priori* could be combined only in pure intuition. That we need some "third something" to justify our combination of subject and predicate independently of experience is in fact the way Kant introduces his problem at the beginning of the Transcendental Analytic.[1] And he makes it clear that he understands by a "third something" some kind of pure intuition, an examination of which would assure us that the subject and predicate concepts of a synthetic *a priori* judgment are combined independently of experience.[2] I shall ask how such a view of the third thing fits Kant's hidden theory of syntheticity; that is, how it can be accommodated to a theory of judgment according to which the problem is not how to combine one concept with another but rather how to combine a concept with an intuition.

The most obvious place to look for an answer to this question is the chapter on schematism in the first *Kritik*.[3] And it is by an examination of this chapter that I want both to explain how Kant distinguishes between kinds of pure intuition and to show that transcendental schemata are the referents of the subject expressions of certain synthetic *a priori* propositions. Yet the explanatory power of the chapter on schematism is dubious just because it is itself beset by obscurities as great as those in the doctrines I want to explain by means of it. We do not have, for example, an acceptable account of the place of the schematism in the argument of the *Kritik*. Nor do we understand what a schema is, since Kant gives us conflicting accounts of schemata. I shall take up both of these problems before trying to relate the doctrine of schematism to Kant's theory of judgment.

---

1. A155 = B194: "Granted, then, that we must advance beyond a given concept in order to compare it synthetically with another, a third something is necessary, as that wherein alone the synthesis of the two concepts can be achieved."

2. *Ibid.*: "What, now, is this third something that is to be the medium of all synthetic judgments? There is only one whole in which all our representations are contained, namely, inner sense and its *a priori* form, time."

3. A137–47 = B176–87.

ᕙ 1 ᕗ

An Obstacle to the Understanding of Schematism

THE MAIN OBSTACLE to an understanding of schematism is found in the argument, first advanced by Green and Prichard and repeated by Warnock, that the theory of schematism conflicts with the results of the Transcendental Deduction.[4] There are many variants of this objection; but they all argue to the conclusion that schematism conflicts with the argument of the Transcendental Deduction; but I single out Warnock's version here as the strongest.[5]

---

4. T. H. Green, *Works* (ed. R. Nettleship [3 vols.; London and New York: Longmans, Green, & Co., 1889–90]), II, 39, argues that schemata are unnecessary because the category and the object to which it is applied have a common source. Cf. H. A. Prichard, *Kant's Theory of Knowledge* (Oxford: Clarendon Press, 1909), Chap. X, *passim*. Cf. also G. J. Warnock, "Concepts and Schematism," *Analysis*, IX (1949), 77–82. The most recent attempt to rescue the theory of schematism from the charge of superfluity without simultaneously conceding the failure of the Transcendental Deduction is made by Eva Schaper in her article, "Kant's Schematism Reconsidered," *Review of Metaphysics*, XVIII (1964), 267–92. She argues there for the existence of two levels in the doctrine of schematism, holding that there is a switch of interest from what she calls a "metaphysics of science and knowledge" to a "metaphysics of experience" (pp. 274–75). I agree that the two concerns which Schaper distinguishes differ in scope. But what Miss Schaper does not explain is how a change in scope in the chapter on schematism could remove the difficulty that either the schematism repeats the work done by the Deduction or that it does what the Deduction set out, but failed, to do. To say that the domain of objects over which schemata range undergoes expansion does not speak to this problem at all. Other commentators (like Ernst Robert Curtius in "Das Schematismus-Kapitel in der *K.r.V.*," *Kant-Studien*, XIX [1916], 338–66) have been fond of pointing out an ambiguity in Kant's use of the concept of subsumption in schematism. Kant uses the term in his *Logik*, para. 58 (*Werke*, VIII, p. 426), to describe the relation of major to minor premise in a syllogism in virtue of a middle term. But the term is used in the chapter on schematism in the first *Kritik* to describe the application of a concept to an intuition. This is easily explained once one sees the distinction I have urged between Kant's explicit and implicit theories of judgment. A synthetic judgment consists, on the implicit theory, in the subsumption of an intuition under a concept.

5. Warnock, *op. cit.*, p. 80.

His objection, briefly, is that Kant wrongly separates our possession of concepts from our ability to use them. To have a concept is not, according to Warnock, like having an object like a gauge which we can carry about and inspect. For we can say that we possess a gauge without knowing how to use it; but we cannot say that we possess a concept without claiming that we know how to use it, to apply it to examples, and to refuse to apply it to objects which do not fall under it.[6] If I claim that I possess a concept but cannot apply it, then it would be legitimate to conclude that I do not in fact possess the concept in question.

If possessing a concept is the same as being able to use it, then the question Kant appears to be asking in the chapter on schematism would appear to be wrongheaded. For he begins that chapter by asking the question that Warnock condemns as nonsensical:

> But pure concepts of understanding being quite heterogeneous from empirical intuitions, and indeed from all sensible intuitions, can never be met with in any intuition. For no one will say that a category, such as that of causality, can be intuited through sense and is itself contained in appearance. How, then, is the *subsumption* of intuitions under pure concepts, the *application* of a category to appearances, possible?[7]

Here Kant appears to assume what Warnock imputes to him. Kant tells us that we possess categorical concepts while asking whether we can apply them to intuitions. When he says that pure concepts apply to but have no referent in appearances, what he appears to be saying is that we have certain concepts in our possession for which we cannot specify any referents at all. Thus, when he asks how appearances can be subsumed under categories, he appears to be asking an inadmissible question.

But the question which Kant asks here is not merely open to philosophical doubts. It appears to conflict with the results at which Kant arrives through the Transcendental Deduction. There he purported to show that claims about objects (as opposed to claims about

6. "To ask how to apply a concept that I have, is to ask how I can use a word that I know how to use" (*ibid.*).
7. A137 = B170.

sense impressions) presuppose our ability to use categories.[8] Part of
what he claims to show is that what distinguishes a manifold of
presentations from an object is our ability to unite the manifold
according to a rule of combination given to us by a concept. Yet the
question with which the chapter on schematism begins (How do we
relate pure concepts to intuitions?) assumes that the Transcendental
Deduction has not done what it purports to do. There Kant claims to
show that we can apply categories to the manifold of sensibility. And
to ask, as he does in the chapter on schematism, how we relate
categories to intuitions is a tacit admission that the Transcendental
Deduction has not answered it. To hold, then, that the Deduction
establishes our right to use pure concepts to synthesize a manifold
makes the question of the chapter on schematism superfluous. For it
will already have been answered.[9]

This, then, is the apparent conflict in the argument of the *Kritik*
which, according to Warnock, results from separating the possession
of concepts from the ability to apply them. If we hold that we can
have concepts in our possession without knowing how to apply them,
then we can be tricked into thinking that we have certain concepts
like categories without knowing how to apply them. We assume, in
other words, that we know what concepts like "cause" and "substance" are. We also assume that we possess them; and only then do
we, according to Warnock, go on to ask how to apply them. But if
we have to ask how to use a concept, we confess that we do not
know what it is and *a fortiori* that we do not possess it. Hence, Kant's
chapter on schematism appears to be an implicit confession of the
failure of his Transcendental Deduction.

The answer to this ancient objection is to admit that the argument
of the Transcendental Deduction *is* incomplete but to deny the conclusion that it is for that reason defective. What Kant sets out to show
in the Transcendental Deduction is that, since the only thing we are
given is a series of presentations, some pure concepts or other are
indispensable if we want to make good our claim that we know

8. Cf. A97 ff. and B138 ff.
9. Cf. Warnock, *op. cit.*, p. 82.

perceptual objects. There are two features of the argument of the Deduction that make it incomplete. First, all that Kant demonstrates there (and all that he needs to demonstrate) is that some kind of procedure for combining presentations enables us to know objects. He is completely silent about what concepts we do use to unite the manifold and how, in particular cases, we establish the right to use these concepts as over against others. Since his argument leaves out any consideration of what concepts in particular we must use if we are to give an adequate analysis of our knowledge of objects, it is necessarily incomplete.

And the Transcendental Deduction is incomplete in a second way. Kant talks of the acts by which the manifold is combined as being, in some sense, temporal. Acts of synthesis go on in time and they are, in some way, related to time and space, which are the conditions of the presentation of objects. But Kant does not ask how a concept, which has very different properties from an intuition, can combine with intuitions to unite a manifold. That there are conceptual elements in the synthesis by which the manifold is united has already been demonstrated, if the argument in the Transcendental Deduction is successful. But Kant is still a long way from explaining how concepts relate to intuitions. So, although Kant intends to show that, if an object is to be known, as over against a series of presentations, part of the synthesis required is supplied by concepts, he is silent about how we relate particular concepts to intuitions.

The Deduction is thus incomplete in at least two ways. But neither incompleteness demonstrates that the Deduction fails to do what Kant meant it to do. To show that Kant has not demonstrated what concepts are needed to combine the manifold is not to expose a weakness in Kant's argument. All he wants to show is that, whatever categories may be required, some kind of combination is necessary for supporting any claim that we know a perceptual object. Nor does the argument fail because Kant does not explain how particular concepts relate to intuitions. For all he needs to establish is that some concepts or other must relate to intuition, not that a particular concept does in fact stand in some relation to intuition. The fact that schematism shows us how particular concepts relate to intuition does indeed show that the Transcendental Deduction is incomplete. It follows from this, however, not that the Transcendental Deduction is a failure, but only that schematism shows for particular concepts what the Deduction shows for concepts in general. Thus Warnock's objection fails because Kant does not make the assumption Warnock imputes to him. Kant does not, that is, assume that we possess any concepts in particular before asking whether we can apply them to experience.

We can thus admit that the Transcendental Deduction must be completed by a theory in which the particular concepts that are required by knowledge of objects are identified. But this provokes the extension of Warnock's objection to the Metaphysical Deduction. It might be objected that the concepts required by knowledge of objects are identified by Kant in the Metaphysical Deduction. Yet, by adding a section on schematism, he nevertheless appears to consider that their applicability to a manifold must still be demonstrated. Has not Warnock's problem broken out again? Either the Metaphysical Deduction is a failure or the chapter on schematism is superfluous.

Let us inquire what Kant sets out to prove in the Metaphysical Deduction. There he makes a classification of judgments according to their logical form. The forms of judgment are called variously "functions of the understanding" and the "function of thought in judgment." [10] I cannot here undertake an analysis of what Kant means by "function." All I wish to point out is that the functions of the understanding give us, on Kant's theory, concepts whose referents are properties of propositions, not of things. Consider, for example, the function of the understanding that appears in Kant's Table of Judgments as the categorical judgment. This is the concept of the subject-predicate relation.[11] What we are given in this concept is not a category because Kant reserves that title for concepts whose referents are things, not propositions. Thus, the category of inherence and subsist-

10. A69 = B94; A70 = B95.
11. A73 = B98: "All relations of thought in judgments are (a) of the predicate to the subject. . . ." The context makes it clear that Kant is discussing the categorical judgment.

ence has a different referent from that of the concept of the subject-predicate relation. The category refers to properties of the manifold. The concept of the subject-predicate relation does not. The difference between a form of the understanding and a category properly so called is that the latter is a way of uniting the manifold while the former is not.[12] To have the concept of the subject-predicate relation is to know something about propositions. To have the concept of inherence and subsistence is to know something about the structure of the manifold.[13]

What I have done is to take the example of the subject-predicate relation to show the important difference between the concepts of the Metaphysical Deduction and those which figure in the chapter on schematism. The same point can be made, *mutatis mutandis*, for all of the concepts identified in the Metaphysical Deduction. To know that a concept is indispensable for the understanding in its activity of judgment is not to know whether that concept has any application to the world. The Metaphysical Deduction purports to show that there are concepts having the former characteristic. But it is powerless to show that these concepts have the latter characteristic. Now Kant does claim that the concepts identified in the Metaphysical Judgment are the same as those which he lists as categories.[14] For this reason, then, it cannot be objected that Kant first assumes that we possess concepts while tacitly admitting that we might not know how to apply them. We both possess and know how to apply the concepts which figure in the Metaphysical Deduction, for we know how to pick out logical relations in the judgments we make. And if these concepts are the same as the concepts which Kant identifies as pure categories, then we

---

12. Cf. A76 = B102.

13. *Ibid.*: "Transcendental logic, on the other hand, has lying before it a manifold of *a priori* sensibility, presented by transcendental aesthetic, as material for the concepts of pure understanding. In the absence of this material those concepts would be without any content, therefore entirely empty." What Kant takes to be an empirical concept he tells us in the *Logik* (*Werke*, VIII, 400 and 401). For a general discussion of Kant's theory of empirical concepts see George Schrader, "Kant's Theory of Concepts," *Kant-Studien*, XLIX (1958), 264–78.

14. A78 = B104.

do possess categorical concepts. But what we do not know is whether there is anything in the manifold of our sensibility which corresponds to them. We can still be said to possess concepts of the categories and to know how to apply them while asking whether there is anything in the manifold corresponding to them. Thus the revised version of the objection considered above does not succeed in showing the superfluity of the chapter on schematism.

Kant's Theories of Schematism

THE THEORY OF SCHEMATISM, whatever other faults it might have, is at least not rendered superfluous either by the results of the Metaphysical Deduction or by those of the Transcendental Deduction. Yet, we are still without an explanation of what a schema is. In the explanation I shall offer, I shall restrict my remarks to those schemata which are related to pure concepts, omitting here consideration of what Kant says about the schemata of empirical concepts.

The *Kritik* contains two conflicting views of transcendental schemata. According to the first view, a schema is a third thing which somehow mediates between a concept and empirical intuitions. Kant introduces the problem in the following way:

In all subsumptions of an object under a concept the representation of the object must be *homogeneous* with the concept; in other words, the concept must contain something which is represented in the object that is to be subsumed under it. This, in fact, is what is meant by the expression, "an object is contained under a concept." Thus the empirical concept of a *plate* is homogeneous with the pure geometrical concept of a *circle*. The roundness which is thought in the latter can be intuited in the former.[15]

15. A137 = B176. This passage contains what to some has appeared to be an error. Cf. Norman Kemp Smith, *A Commentary to Kant's* Critique of Pure Reason (New York: Humanities Press, 1962), pp. 335 ff. When Kant discusses the homogeneity between concept and object, he gives as his example the homogeneity of the concept of a plate with the *concept* of a circle ("mit dem reinen geometrischen eines Zirkels . . ."), whereas the context demands that he supply an example of the homogeneity of a concept and an *object*.

All that Kant so far requires of a schema is that it be homogeneous (*gleichartig*) with the object and the concept through which the object is known. This requirement leaves it an entirely open question whether homogeneity is to be analyzed as a relation of similarity between concept and object or rather as an entity which has properties of both concept and object. Kant opts for the latter alternative when he says:

> Obviously there must be some third thing, which is homogeneous on the one hand with the category, and on the other hand with the appearance, and which thus makes the application of the former to the latter possible. This mediating representation must be pure, that is, void of all empirical content, and yet at the same time, while it must in one respect be *intellectual,* it must in another be *sensible.* Such a representation is the *transcendental schema.*[16]

The requirement of homogeneity is thus met by introducing a new entity (called a *vermittelnde Vorstellung*) into the discussion. It is neither an intuition nor a concept. It cannot be an intuition because an intuition is a particular and is moreover entirely sensuous. Kant tells us that all intuitions and only intuitions are particular when he argues in the Aesthetic that space and time (the only pure intuitions we have) are particulars, not concepts. Any spatial-temporal appearance would consequently be particular as well.

If a schema is not a particular, it cannot be sensuous. This follows from what Kant says about sensibility. He defines sensibility by reference to what is received as spatial and temporal.[17] So, on the third-thing view of schemata, a schema cannot be an intuition. For an intuition is both particular and sensuous. But a schema can be neither.

Still less can a schema be a concept. We presumably need schemata because pure concepts are not homogeneous with intuitions. And a schema is introduced to supply a pure concept with something that it lacks. But if a schema could be a concept, then a schema would be merely another mark or note (*Merkmal*) which we add to the definition of a pure concept. And Kant is careful to point out that no

16. A138 = B177.
17. Cf. B35 and B36. For the argument that all intuitions are particulars see B40 and B48.

addition of concepts to a definition of a pure concept could show us how we can apply that concept to appearances. For the problem he sets himself at the beginning of schematism is not how we *define* concepts like "substance" and "causality" but rather how we can supply them with intuitions.[18] The conclusion Kant draws from his consideration of the requirements of schematism is not, as we might expect, that a schema is neither a concept nor an intuition but rather that it is both. This is an immediate consequence of his demand that a schema be both intellectual and sensuous.

This inference is plainly suspect. But I do not think that it is based on a misinterpretation of the first part of the chapter on schematism. To show this, let me compare the reading I have just given of that section with the reading given by H. J. Paton, one of Kant's most sympathetic commentators. Paton interprets schemata as "certain universal characteristics corresponding to the categories."[19] Yet such an interpretation is beset with difficulties. If a schema is said to be a universal characteristic, it would seem to follow that it is a concept, since only concepts can be universal for Kant. But Paton argues that these universal characteristics are not categories but rather that they correspond to categories. This will not do either. If transcendental schemata are not concepts but only correspond to concepts, then they can only be intuitions. But this Paton implicitly denies when he asserts that schemata are universal characteristics. For no intuition could be a universal characteristic simply because an intuition is a particular, not a universal. The reading Paton gives of the passage reflects the same divided view that I have found in Kant. His interpretation supports the *tertium quid* view, according to which transcendental schemata are both intuitional and conceptual just because they cannot be either.

Let us, however, ignore the illicit inference behind the *tertium quid* view of schemata. That theory is still embarrassed by both a philosophical and a textual difficulty. The philosophical difficulty, baldly put, is that the view is self-contradictory. For Kant clearly

18. A137 = B176 and A138 = B177.
19. H. J. Paton, *Kant's Metaphysic of Experience* (2 vols.; London: George Allen & Unwin, 1951), II, 28; cf. pp. 19, 22, and 29.

regards ". . . is a particular" and ". . . is a universal" as mutually exclusive predicates. True, when he talks about a schema as a third thing, he does not say that it is both universal and particular but only that it is both intellectual and sensuous.[20] This is not enough, however, to rescue the third-thing view of a schema from contradiction. For Kant, all particulars are sensuous in that they must be either pure or empirical intuitions; similarly, all universals are intellectual, since Kant identifies universals with concepts.[21] So the contradiction emerges when Kant introduces an entity that is both universal and particular. When I say that to conceive of a schema as a third thing which is both universal and particular is contradictory, I am not denying that entities can be *composites* of universals and particulars. For composites are not entities that are universal and particular in the same respect. They result from the combination of entities which are universal and those which are particular. The trouble is, however, that schemata understood as third things are not composites but are independent entities about which Kant is forced to say that they are both universal and particular. And this generates the contradiction.

There is also a powerful textual argument against the *tertium quid* theory: Kant gives us quite a different view of schemata in another passage. At A141 = B180 Kant introduces the following theory:

> The schema of the triangle can exist nowhere but in thought. It is a rule of synthesis of the imagination, in respect to pure figures in space. Still less is an object of experience or its image ever adequate to the empirical concept; for this latter always stands in immediate relation to the schema of imagination, as a rule for the determination of our intuition, in accordance with some specific universal concept. The concept "dog" signifies a rule acording to which my imagination can delineate the figure of a four-footed animal in a general manner, without limitation to any single determinate figure such as experience, or any possible image that I can represent *in concreto*, actually presents.

Immediately following this passage is a statement of the theory in terms of transcendental schemata:

20. A138 = B177.
21. Cf. *Logik*, paras. 1 and 2 (*Werke*, Vol. VIII).

On the other hand, the schema of a *pure* concept of understanding can never be brought into any image whatsoever. It is simply the pure synthesis, determined by a rule of that unity, in accordance with concepts, to which the category gives expression. . . . It is a transcendental product of imagination, a product which concerns the determination of inner sense in general according to conditions of its form (time). . . .[22]

This diverges sharply from the third-thing view of a schema. The task which was previously to be performed by an entity which was both universal and particular is now discharged by a procedure for producing intuitions of a certain kind. On this new view, a rule would be a prescription for producing an image in either pure or empirical intuition. And a rule is not an intuition: a rule tells us how to construct something in intuition but is not itself an intuition. Thus the rule theory rescues the general theory of schematism from contradiction. For we are no longer constrained to assume entities to which incompatible properties are assigned.

But the rule theory conflicts with what Kant says elsewhere. Kant holds that pure concepts have no image or sense presentations that correspond to them.[23] Yet if there are no images or examples which can be generated by applying the rules attached to categories, then how can such rules ever prescribe a procedure for determining inner sense in general, as Kant claims that they do? Either the pure concepts determine the conditions of our sensibility or they do not. If they do, then it must be the case that pure categories have intuitional representations that correspond to them. If they do not, then pure categories cannot be schematized, for the schema is, according to the rule theory, a rule which can generate objects which fall under these concepts.

But the rule theory of transcendental schemata is still beset by a problem: Either a category cannot be schematized at all, or, if it can be schematized, then it must be the case that pure concepts do, after all, have elements in sensibility which correspond to them. If there is no representation in the manifold corresponding to the category, then how can we find out what counts as a referent of a pure concept? How

22. A142 = B181.
23. A88 = B120; A137 = B176.

are we to know that what we have constructed is an example of the pure concept which we seek to schematize? The rule for generating images of pure concepts presupposes that we know what would count as an image of a pure concept. But then a schema cannot be a rule unless we already have a concept of a schema which is the kind of entity generated by applying the rule. What this entity is and how it is best characterized are questions that I leave aside here. Whatever the entity is, that there be such an entity is required by Kant's position that rules are schemata because they generate images in intuition. The rule theory of schematism fails, then, because we cannot know what to construct in intuition unless we already know what the construct is like. And this is just the question that a theory of schematism is meant to answer.

The philosophical objection I have been raising to the rule theory is generated by two claims that Kant makes about pure concepts and sensibility. On the one hand, Kant repeatedly says that pure concepts contain no mark or note (*Merkmal*) to which something in our sensuous manifold corresponds: Pure concepts are devoid of sensuous content. On the other hand, Kant says that a schema can supply the element which the pure concept lacks, for he says that a schema can make the pure concept homogeneous with our manifold. And this generates the problem which the rule theory cannot solve. If a schema is a rule, all we are given is a directive for the application of the pure concept. But if the pure concept lacks all homogeneity with the sensuous manifold, the addition of a rule will not remedy this defect unless we supplement the rule-governed pure concept with the concept of an entity that does have something in our manifold corresponding to it. And then the problem of schematism—finding something in sensibility that corresponds to the pure concept—will have been solved. This will, in turn, make the addition of a rule unnecessary. I am not denying that schematism does away with the necessity for rules in the application of concepts. What I am denying is that the addition of rules to pure concepts alone suffices to bring these concepts any closer to sensibility.

The second theory of schematism contained in the *Kritik* is objectionable, then, both on textual and philosophical grounds. The textual ground is that, according to the rule theory, a schema is a concept: It is a procedure for constructing something in intuition. But if a schema is a concept, then it conflicts with another view of Kant's, according to which no pure concept can have any image or sense presentation corresponding to it in intuition. And if this is the case, it would follow that the schema of a pure category could not be a rule for constructing anything in intuition.

The philosophical reason for objecting to the rule theory as it is stated in the text is no less fatal. If the pure concept does not have images or examples corresponding to it in intuition, then we will not know what to count as an example of any pure concept. For if a schema is a way of applying the category to intuition, we will not know what is to count as an object falling under the concept unless we already have a concept by which we can recognize the entity offered as an example of the category. Thus as long as we conceive of the schema of a concept as a rule, we must have a concept of the result of applying that rule in order to know when we have correctly applied the concept which we are trying to schematize. But the concept of the result of applying a schema is different from the schema itself. Hence the philosophical difficulty with the rule theory is that it presupposes a quite different theory of schematism according to which a schema is the concept of the result of applying a rule. And this is completely absent from the rule theory as it is stated in the chapter on schematism.

There is a way of rehabilitating the rule theory which has been impressively defended by R. P. Wolff. He denies that it is the task of a rule understood as a transcendental schema to generate any kind of intuition. Generating intuitions is the job of first-level rules, which we associate with empirical concepts. Categories are not rules but "types of rules. They bear the same relation to empirical schemata that empirical schemata bear to images." [24] Empirical schemata are rules

---

24. R. P. Wolff, *Kant's Theory of Mental Activity* (Cambridge: Harvard University Press, 1963), p. 212; cf. pp. 206–23. For another, less fortunate, statement of the rule theory see Ernst Robert Curtius, *op. cit.*

about the combination of intuitions. But a transcendental schema is a rule about the rules governing combinations of intuitions.[25]

I can understand what it means to associate representations with one another in sequences which are given to us by rules for empirical concepts. But what is it that we are supposed to construct when we are given rules about rules? Wolff contrasts the two kinds of rules by reference to pottery-making:

> Suppose that a visitor to the pottery asks the general question, How does one make earthenware? The potter may answer somewhat as follows: First place a certain amount of clay on the wheel; then turn the wheel at the proper speed, shaping the clay in the desired manner; etc., etc. Now not even the quickest pupil could possibly learn from this description how to make earthenware, for the potter is not giving the rules for bowl-making, plate-making, or vase-making. He is really giving a rule-type with whose use the pupil can construct pottery-making rules. This rule about rules, or second-order rule, if formulated as a rule, might read: First lay it down how much clay shall be placed on the wheel; then prescribe the speed at which the wheel shall be turned; then specify the shaping movements of the hands; and so forth.[26]

The relation between a second-order rule about pottery-making and rules for making pottery is just the relation, according to Wolff, that holds between transcendental schemata and empirical concepts. Schemata tell us something about concepts, not about things to which these concepts refer. Thus a category has been schematized, according to Wolff, when we have shown how it prescribes rules for using empirical concepts.

Wolff's version of the rule theory can be made clear by illustrating how it applies to the concept of substance. When Kant schematizes the category of substance, Wolff is saying, what Kant does is to list rules governing the application of any empirical concept to the manifold of sensibility. Consider, for example, the empirical concepts of "table" and "chair." I apply these concepts to the manifold when I pick out certain presentations and join them together. Learning to apply concepts like these is largely a matter of learning what to

25. Wolff, *op. cit.*, p. 212.
26. *Ibid.*, pp. 212 f.

exclude from the manifold of presentations and how to unite the remainder. The concept of substance enters here in the following way. When we are given general directions about applying concepts like "table" and "chair," we have schematized the category of substance. Such general directions would require that the presentations which are selected from the manifold be joined to form an object which endures through space and time. But such directions would tell us something about how to apply concepts of empirical objects. They would not tell us how to find anything in the world which corresponds to what we think in the category of substance.

This version of the rule theory breaks down on an ambiguity. Exactly what do rules about rules tell us? Here there are only two alternatives. They can tell us something about the manifold to be combined, or they can tell us something about the structure of the rules by which we combine the manifold. Let us consider these alternatives in turn. First of all, it is obvious that what Wolff calls a second-order rule could not tell us something about the manifold. If it did, it would not be a rule *about rules* at all. What a second-order rule would tell us if it governed our relation to the manifold would have to pertain to our behavior toward a part of the manifold which would not be covered by the empirical or first-order rules which prescribe our behavior toward a manifold. But then it would be appropriate to ask what part of the manifold would be governed by the second-order rule which would not be governed by the totality of first-order rules. If there were some elements in the manifold which would require second-order rules, then such rules would not be about other *rules* at all; and then it would follow that they would simply not qualify as what Wolff calls second-order rules.

Suppose, however, that second-order rules tell us something about the logical structure that first-order rules must have in order to count as rules. This is, I think, the more plausible way of putting Wolff's suggestion. But if this is what he is saying, then it falls apart upon very little examination. This can be seen by paying attention to the difference between categories and other concepts. If a schematized category were interpreted as a rule directing us to form other rules in a certain way, a category would be equated with what Kant calls a function of judgment. A function of judgment is for Kant the logical structure of a kind of judgment. When I say, for example, that a judgment is categorical or that it is hypothetical, what I am distinguishing is two functions of judgment. Thus the concept of such a function is a concept of the relation between other concepts in a judgment.[27] A category, on the other hand, is a concept of the relation, not between concepts, but between intuitions.[28] The concept of inherence and subsistence is for Kant a concept of the relation between permanence and temporal change. It is not a concept of a relation between elements in judgment *about* permanence and change. A schematized category cannot, therefore, be a rule about how to form rules. And it cannot be this because a schematized category is not a concept about the relation of other concepts to one another but rather a concept about the relation of things to one another. We are, then, left with the problem I mentioned before examining Wolff's suggestion: A rule cannot give us the full story about a Kantian schema because Kant must show what in experience corresponds to a category; and no amount of discourse about the structure of other parts of our discourse will suffice to show what kinds of objects fall under the categories that Kant lists.

The failure of both the third-thing theory and the rule theory does not, however, force the abandonment of the entire theory of schematism. There are, I believe, the roots of a third theory of transcendental schemata in Kant, according to which a transcendental schema is neither a rule nor some third thing but rather an intuition. This is not, to be sure, a view of transcendental schemata that Kant openly adopts. But I shall argue that, for purely structural reasons, he is committed to it. Such a view is suggested, first of all, by the way in which Kant talks about schematizing empirical concepts. The view

27. Beginning at A70 = B95, Kant gives what he takes to be an exhaustive list of the functions of judgment. At A72 = B98 he discusses the categorical and hypothetical forms of the judgment as functions.

28. At A79 = B105 Kant gives the list of categories; his discussion of the category of subsistence and inherence is given in the first Analogy. I reserve comment on his discussion until Chapter Five.

also explains the schemata Kant gives for pure concepts. And, finally, that a transcendental schema must be a pure intuition is a consequence of what Kant means by demonstrating the objective validity of a concept.

Consider the kind of proof Kant demands for showing that a concept is possible. In the Postulates of Empirical Thought Kant distinguishes between showing that a concept is possible and showing that it has objective validity:

> A concept which contains a synthesis is to be regarded as empty and as not related to any object, if this synthesis does not belong to experience either as being derived from it, in which case it is an *empirical concept*, or as being an *a priori* condition upon which experience in general in its formal aspect rests, in which case it is a *pure concept*. In the latter case it still belongs in experience, inasmuch as its object is to be met with only in experience. . . . It is, indeed, a necessary logical condition that a concept of the possible must not contain any contradiction; but this is not by any means sufficient to determine the objective reality of the concept, that is, the possibility of such an object as is thought through the concept.[29]

Applying this distinction to transcendental schemata, Kant says:

> Only through the fact that these concepts express *a priori* the relations of perceptions in every experience, do we know their objective reality, that is, their transcendental truth, and this, indeed, independently of experience, though not independently of all relation to the form of an experience in general, and to the synthetic unity in which alone objects can be empirically known.[30]

To show that a concept is objectively valid as distinct from internally consistent is to exhibit the object of the concept in intuition. What Kant is insisting here is that a question of the right to use a concept is a question of our ability to give it an object.[31] And pure concepts, no less than empirical concepts, must be given objects in experience. Kant is not holding that pure concepts are objectively valid despite the fact that they have nothing corresponding to them in experience. They are objectively valid because they have a special kind of object which

29. A220 = B267.
30. A222 = B269.
31. B22.

Kant calls the relation of perceptions which are encountered in every experience.

This same concern is present in the argument of schematism, where Kant says:

> For we have seen that concepts are altogether impossible, and can have no meaning, if no object is given for them, or at least for the elements of which they are composed. They cannot, therefore, be viewed as applicable to things in themselves, independent of all question as to whether and how these may be given to us.[32]

In other words: Part of what we look for when we look for a schema is an object. Once we have shown that such an object does fall under a concept, we have succeeded in showing that the concept in question has objective validity.[33]

Kant's procedure of finding out whether a concept is meaningful by showing that it has objects falling under it can be further illustrated by reference to his theory of empirical concepts. Empirical concepts can, to be sure, be schematized more easily than *a priori* concepts. And I do not want to deny the significant difference between the two kinds of schemata. It is, however, equally important to understand that Kant's theory of what schematism is does not change when he discusses empirical concepts. Consider what Kant says when he introduces the example of the relation of homogeneity between the plate and my concept of it. At $A137 = B176$ he says this about the relation between the two: "Thus the empirical concept of a *plate* is homogeneous with the pure geometrical concept of a *circle*. The roundness which is thought in the latter can be intuited in the former."

Kant offers this as an example of schematizing an empirical concept. What he demands here is an explanation of how we can know that what we are presented with in intuition does in fact fall under the concept of "plate." This much should be clear from what he says in the passage immediately preceding $A137 = B176$. For he asks there how we can subsume an object under a concept. And the answer he

32. $A139 = B178$.
33. Cf. $A139 = B178$; $A245 = B302$, footnote; $A596 = B624$, footnote.

gives for empirical concepts is that we must show that there is an object in intuition which corresponds to the concept we want to schematize. Thus, in the case of an empirical concept like that of a plate, we schematize it when we can show that a note in the concept of a plate (namely, the property of roundness) can be presented to us in intuition. On Kant's theory of the concept, this question is bound to arise. When a concept is conceived as an aggregate of notes by which features of objects are recognized, we cannot understand how to apply a concept until we have singled out elements in experience to which the marks in our concept stand in a relation of correspondence. It is important to note that Kant does not restrict these requirements to empirical concepts but in fact extends them to cover *a priori* concepts. Thus, at the very beginning of the chapter on schematism he says: "In *all* subsumptions of an object under a concept the representation of the object must be *homogeneous* with the concept. . . . This, in fact, is what is meant by the expression, 'an object is contained under a concept.' " [34] An object cannot be subsumed under a concept until we can show that there is something in the object in virtue of which we can subsume it under the concept. To show this is to show both that there is a mark in the concept and that there is something in the object which corresponds to that mark.

When Kant points out that a pure concept is not homogeneous with appearance, he is, to be sure, denying that any *appearance* (*Erscheinung* = empirical intuition) can correspond to the marks contained in a pure concept. But it does not follow from this point (and we have just seen how Kant does not take it to follow) that a pure concept need be homogeneous with nothing at all in intuition. The requirement of homogeneity is placed on both empirical and pure concepts. The difference is that, in the case of pure concepts, we must look to something other than appearances for the correlate of a concept. In discussing Kant's distinction between empirical and pure concepts, I argued that, just as empirical intuition provides objects for empirical concepts, so pure intuition can provide objects for pure

34. A137 = B176. The first emphasis is added.

concepts. Hence, the distinguishing characteristic of a pure concept is not that it has no correlate at all in intuition but rather that its correlate is found in pure intuition.

This interpretation of transcendental schemata is given additional support by what Kant says in his essay *Ueber die Fortschritte der Metaphysik seit Leibniz und Wolff*, where he holds the following:

> Knowledge is a judgment from which a concept emerges that has objective validity. . . . One of the two modes of representation alone does not by itself constitute knowledge; and, if it is to provide synthetic *a priori* knowledge, there must be intuitions as well as *a priori* concepts.[35]

What does this passage tell us? For one thing, it tells us that a synthetic judgment *a priori* consists in the assertion that intuitions fall under pure concepts. And this is exactly what we should expect Kant to say if the conclusions of the preceding chapters are sound. More important, however, is the point that the existence of such judgments assumes that there are *a priori* intuitions falling under pure concepts. The possibility of synthetic judgments *a priori* depends, therefore, on the existence of intuitions which fall under pure concepts.

We may thus infer that the requirement of homogeneity with an object is laid down for both pure and empirical concepts. How else can a pure concept have what Kant calls objective validity unless it can be shown that there are pure intuitions falling under it?[36] This much should be clear from the discussion of the passage from the Postulates of Empirical Thought in the first *Kritik*. And it is confirmed by what Kant says here. For, if we cannot show that there are pure intuitions corresponding to the categories, we cannot show that there are any

---

35. *Werke*, VIII, 244–45.
36. Cf. A145 = B185: "Also sind die Schemate der reinen Verstandesbegriffe die wahren und einzigen Bedingungen, diesen eine Beziehung auf Objekte, mithin Bedeutung zu verschaffen." Cf. also *Über die Fortschritte der Metaphysik*, *Werke*, VIII, 260: "Einen reinen Begriff des Verstandes, als an einem Gegenstande möglicher Erfahrung denkbar vorstellen, heisst, ihm objektive Realität verschaffen, und überhaupt, ihn darstellen. . . . Diese Handlung, wenn die objektive Realität dem Begriff geradezu (directe) durch die demselben korrespondierende Anschauung zugeteilt, d.i. dieser unmittelbar dargestellt wird, heisst der Schematism. . . ."

synthetic judgments *a priori*. Thus the structural reason for the view that a transcendental schema is a pure intuition comes to this: Given Kant's requirement that the meaningfulness of a concept is demonstrated by exhibiting an object which falls under it, the only kind of object a pure concept could have consistent with its status in Kant's theory is a pure intuition. And to show that there are such intuitions is the avowed purpose of the chapter on schematism. For Kant expressly equates a demonstration of homogeneity of concept and object with a demonstration that there are objects contained under a concept.[37]

The structural reasons for interpreting a transcendental schema as a pure intuition do not, however, stand alone. They are confirmed by the schemata that Kant in fact associates with pure concepts. Here I cannot give a full discussion of the entire list of schemata Kant introduces. I consider only the schema for the pure concept of substance.[38] Kant holds that the schema of the pure concept of substance is time itself, for which he gives the following argument. To measure any kind of change, I must single out an element which is permanent in order to discover that any change is time itself. If we assume that time itself changes, the change can only take place within another time. So the assumption that time changes presupposes a time that does not change in order that it can be measured. But time itself is a pure intuition; consequently, the schema of substance is a pure intuition.

For the moment I omit asking whether it makes sense to say that time itself does not change or whether, even if we can make out a case for treating time as a changeless entity, it follows that time itself is the correlate of substance. All I want to point out is that what Kant chooses to call a schema is neither a kind of third thing nor a rule. Time itself is obviously not a rule of any kind. It does, of course, give us a manifold: there are particular time spans which are brought

---

37. A137 = B176: "In allen Subsumtionen eines Gegenstandes unter einen Begriff muss die Vorstellung des ersteren mit der letzteren gleichartig sein, d.i. der Begriff muss dasjenige enthalten, was in dem darunter zu subsumierenden Gegenstande vorgestellt wird, *denn das bedeutet eben der Ausdruck: ein Gegenstand sei unter einem Begriffe enthalten*" (emphasis added).

38. A143 = B183.

together when we talk about any object enduring from one time to another. And this manifold, like any other manifold, is combined according to a rule. But time itself cannot in any sense *be* the rule; for it is what the rule combines. Nor is time a kind of third thing—something that is both sensuous and intellectual. Since it is an intuition, a schema is entirely sensuous. Rules for combining time spans are added to our apprehension of time by the understanding. But rules are *added* and are thus not parts of time itself.

❦ 3 ❦

Schemata and Pure Concepts

THAT SCHEMATA are transcendental time determinations is, I have argued, the consequence of the general requirements Kant lays down for a schema. What is to qualify as a transcendental schema is the object which falls under the pure concept. Such an object cannot be empirical because there is nothing in an empirical object which corresponds to a pure concept; hence, it must be pure. And the pure objects which can fall under pure concepts are characteristics of pure intuition. This theory of schematism also accounts for what both the third-thing and the rule theories were intended to explain. A characteristic of pure intuition can be a mediating representation because it stands between pure concepts and empirical intuitions: By showing how the pure concept has a corresponding element in pure intuition Kant can show how that concept can serve as a rule of synthesis for our manifold and, further, how that rule of synthesis can underlie all other rules of synthesis for our manifold. A rule of synthesis that governs the combination of pure intuition will be a condition of the application of any other rule just because pure intuition is itself a condition of the apprehension of any object in our manifold. The third-thing view of schematism is an attempt to explain how schemata can have these characteristics; but, as we have seen, it failed because the explanation it offered consisted in assigning mutually exclusive predicates to schemata.

The rule theory also has its place in the conception of a schema as a transcendental time determination. The fatal defect of the rule theory was that it presupposed another theory of schematism according to which Kant could supply objects for pure concepts. For the rule theory provided only that a schema was a rule for the construction of objects. But the existence of such a rule presupposes that we already have succeeded in discovering what is to count as the object which it constructs. And this discovery, since it would consist in specifying the characteristic of objects in virtue of which they fall under pure concepts, would be the solution to the problem Kant sets himself in the chapter on schematism. But the rule theory, if it is not the whole truth about schematism, is at least an indispensable part of that theory. It is not enough to specify an object which falls under a pure concept. What must also be specified is the way in which we synthesize that object. And this is supplied by a rule for synthesizing the objects which correspond to pure concepts in our manifold.

Thus the theory according to which transcendental schemata are either pure intuitions or characteristics of pure intuition can accommodate both the rule and the third-thing theories. And such a theory is, I have argued, present in the chapter on schematism. But this raises a question about the relation of pure concepts to their schemata. Kant describes this relation when he says that schemata "first realise the categories" and that they are restricting conditions of the categories.[39] But can schemata restrict categories? On the theory of categories assumed in the doctrine of schematism, there can be no such restriction. What Kant is presenting for schematism is the pure concepts of the understanding.[40] These are the concepts which appear as the logical functions of unity in judgment; and they are the same concepts as those which are concepts of an object in general.[41] Thus the concept of subject and predicate is the same concept as that of substance and accident: What makes them the same concept is that they

39. $A146 = B186$.
40. $A137 = B176$.
41. $A95 = B128$: "The categories . . . are concepts of an object in general." Cf. $B150$; $A289 = B346$; $A247 = B304$.

are both the concept of that which is always subject and never a predicate. But the schema of this concept is permanence in time.[42] The concept of the hypothetical judgment is, similarly, the same concept as that of causation—something from which something else can be inferred.[43] And the schema of this concept is "that which is real, upon which, given it, something else invariably follows." [44]

But the schema of a pure concept cannot restrict it. Suppose that the schema of a pure concept is, as I have argued, a pure intuition or a characteristic of pure intuition: It is thus an object which falls under the concept and must therefore contain something that is represented in the concept under which it falls. Yet this is precisely what a schema cannot do. The pure concepts for which Kant seeks schemata can contain nothing which is represented in the concepts under which they fall. Pure concepts refer to an object in general and are thus compatible with any form of sensibility. Thus to say that our intuition provides schemata which fall under pure concepts violates the requirement that pure concepts must contain a representation corresponding to these objects. The doctrine of schematism, then, faces the following dilemma. If the pure concepts contain elements which are intuited in the objects falling under them, then they are not the same concepts which are catalogued in Kant's categories. But if the pure concepts do not contain representations which refer to elements found in our sensibility, then they cannot be schematized at all because they will not be homogeneous with our manifold. Thus we must either abandon the view that pure concepts are being schematized or abandon the view that pure concepts can be schematized.

This is a problem about the application of metaphysical concepts to experience which goes to the core of a principal contention of Kant, preserved by the tradition of Kant commentary, that all metaphysical propositions consist of a combination of pure concepts.[45] I wish to argue that such a view of what a metaphysical proposition is neither

42. A143 = B183.
43. A243 = B301.
44. A143 = B183.
45. *Prolegomena,* para. I (*Werke*, IV, 13 f.).

fits Kant's own critical principles nor is philosophically viable. That it is not philosophically tenable can be shown by reflecting on the notion of a pure concept. Such a concept is for Kant independent, not only of a particular experience, but also of any experience at all. It contains nothing which refers to intuition.[46] And if this is so, then no synthetic proposition in metaphysics can ever be verified. It cannot be shown that any object falls under that concept because it is impossible to show any object in our manifold which corresponds to the elements in the metaphysical proposition. Thus, as long as metaphysical propositions are treated in this way, they will not be decidable at all.

There are two ways by which one might try to make this claim philosophically viable. Both of them consist in trying to show that a different exegesis can be given of the relation of a category to the objects falling under it. Neither one of them succeeds; but it is important for my purposes to see exactly why they are not successful. The first such effort might run as follows. It begins by insisting that a pure category can be applied to our manifold without the addition of any element to the category which would distinguish the category conceptually from the schematized category. So far, then, it is consistent with Kant's claim that the pure categories can be schematized. But there is a second claim: that the object which falls under the category is not a schema but rather an empirical object of the sort that we are given in empirical intuition. To schematize a category is to show that all the objects of our manifold fall under it, not that a particular object falls under the category as representing in intuition what is thought in the category. Thus it would not be necessary to provide another conceptual representation, added to the category, which marks out a corresponding element in intuition. A schema would not be an object but rather a condition for the application of categories to objects. And the condition would not itself *be* an object but only an element in the manifold the existence of which constitutes a necessary condition for the application of pure concepts to the objects in our manifold.

46. *Ibid.*

If this were a viable exegesis, then the problem I am raising about Kant's view of a metaphysical proposition would evaporate. A metaphysical proposition could be composed of pure concepts but could be verified by showing that all empirical objects fall under the concepts involved as long as certain conditions are present in intuition. And we would have to give up the view that a schema of a pure concept is an object in intuition which would have to exhibit an element which is thought in the category. The schema is not the object which falls under the pure concept; what falls under that concept are empirical objects, while the schema is merely the condition of applying the category to those objects.

This account of the relation between categories and schemata creates more problems in the text than it solves. For one thing, such a view would ignore the requirement which Kant makes of a schema that the objects falling under a concept must be homogeneous with the concept. If the schema were only a condition for applying the concept to intuition, then there would be nothing in an empirical object in virtue of which it falls under the concept. The analysis of an empirical object would yield an enumeration of sense presentations ordered in a certain way. And if there were nothing in the analysis that corresponded to the category, then how could the category apply to such objects? Even if we consider that the forms of our sensibility are necessary conditions for the application of categories to the manifold, this will still not fulfill the requirement of homogeneity. For although it is the case that the forms of our sensibility do function in this way, it does not follow that they contain anything corresponding to the categories that we seek to apply to them, in which case we will be unable to explain, as Kant wants to explain, how the categories are realized in our manifold. And so this view of schematism, which purports to avoid the problem I am raising about the relation between schema and category, must be rejected.

But there is another way in which my problem might be avoided. We could say that there is, after all, an element in the pure concept which is intuited in the object falling under the category. Two examples will illustrate this alternative. The concept which Kant calls the category of substance refers to that which is a subject but never a predicate.[47] And similarly, when we entertain the concept of cause, what we are entertaining is the concept of something from which something else necessarily follows.[48] Both of these concepts refer, as they stand, to an object in general. But when they are applied to our manifold, then they refer to such objects as the permanent in time, in the case of substance, or to necessary succession according to a rule, in the case of cause. This alternative supplies the part of the pure concept which corresponds to an element in our manifold without forcing the admission that the categories themselves must be altered if they are to apply to our manifold.

And yet the element which is, according to this interpretation, contained in the pure concept is not the element which can correspond to the schema for our manifold. Consider again the examples of substance and cause. And let us assume that we do entertain the concept of that which is subject but never predicate when we think of substance and the concept of something from which the existence of something follows when we think of the concept of cause. The object of the former concept may be the permanent through time in our manifold. But our concept of the permanent through time is not the same as our concept of that which is subject but never predicate. All that the former concept allows us to conceive is an entity which cannot relate to another by being either predicable of or present in it. But this does not limit our choice of perceptual particulars to those which endure through time. We can count as a particular any entity that is subject but never predicate and still choose to analyze perceptual particulars as instantaneous. Hence the concept of substance cannot contain the same concept as that of the schema.

And the same can be shown for the concept of cause. When we entertain that concept, Kant tells us, we entertain a concept of something from which something else necessarily follows. And the schema of this concept is succession according to a rule. But these concepts are different. The pure category of cause refers to a relation

47. A235 = B289.
48. A90–91 = B123–24.

between two entities one of which is deducible from another, while the concept of the schema refers to a relation between two entities which is contingent. Thus the concept of cause cannot contain an element which is realized in the schema. For the relation of succession according to a rule is contingent, while the relation between two entities one of which is deducible from the other is not.

I have considered only two examples of the kind of relation which, on the view of schematism under consideration, must hold between a category and its schema. And such a relation does not hold. But the point can be separated from the peculiarities of these two examples and generalized to cover any concept which Kant calls a pure category. The claim that is fundamental to the view under consideration is that a pure category contains an element which refers to an element which corresponds in our manifold to what is thought in the pure category. That there can be no such element unless the pure category is altered from manifold to manifold can be shown as follows. No element in our manifold will be shared by any other possible manifold. This is just a consequence of the definition of our manifold as peculiar to our sensibility, from which we can infer that any other arbitrarily selected manifold will be different from ours. Otherwise it would be identical with the manifold we have. And so, given any element in our manifold, there can be no element in the pure category which is a concept of that element. If there were, then the concept of that element would be a concept of an element which is peculiar to our manifold, and it would follow that the pure category would not be the concept of an object in general. The conclusion is that the alternative under consideration cannot show how a pure category can contain an element corresponding to the schemata of our manifold without ceasing to be a pure category.

The problem with which we began this section, then, remains unsolved. A pure category cannot be schematized. That it can is a claim which is at variance with the requirement of schematism. This in turn will force us to alter our view of the relation between schemata and categories. A transcendental schema is, as I have already argued, a characteristic of pure intuition. But finding these characteristics does not exhaust the procedure of schematism. The concepts of these schemata must supplement the categories. To apply a category to our manifold, then, involves both searching for the appropriate concepts with which to supplement the pure categories as well as locating the objects which correspond to these enriched concepts in our intuition. Now Kant's own description of what he is doing in schematism is not this specific. But it is, I believe, what he actually does when he schematizes the pure categories. The main textual evidence for the claim is that it explains what the chapter on schematism is doing in the *Kritik*. Consider the relation of the chapter on schematism to the remainder of the Analytic of Principles. Kant first arrives at a list of objects which he considers to be homogeneous with the pure concepts in our manifold. Such a list shows how pure concepts apply to the manifold we have. But then he continues to offer separate proofs for each of the schematized categories, arguing that each is necessarily and universally valid of our manifold. Now if Kant were merely discussing the pure categories in the Analytic of Principles, the series of separate proofs he gives of their applicability to our manifold would be completely superfluous. If the only thing Kant wants to prove is that the pure categories are applicable to the manifold, he will have proved that much by the combined results of the Metaphysical and the Transcendental Deductions. To show that our manifold stands under the categories, it is enough to show, first, that our ability to think any manifold is the result of possessing the lists of concepts identified in the Metaphysical Deduction and, secondly, that our manifold presupposes functions of synthesis for us to know the objects presented in that manifold. A separate proof for each category would simply be out of place, for we would already have the proof which is sought.

But Kant does not argue in that way. And the only way in which it might be explained that he does offer a separate proof for each category is that the concepts whose applicability to our manifold he is seeking to establish are different from the ones which he enumerates in the Metaphysical Deduction. What Kant seeks to do in the Analytic of Principles is to show that the schematized categories are universally and necessarily applicable to experience.[49]

The outcome of this analysis of the relation between schematism and the pure categories is that we must alter our view of the kinds of concepts which Kant takes to compose a synthetic *a priori* proposition in metaphysics. Kant often enough tells us that such propositions are composed only of pure concepts. But this rests on the assumption that a pure concept can be schematized without adding another concept—the concept of the schema—to the category. And this assumption, while it is in part present in the chapter on schematism, is false. The paradigm of a synthetic *a priori* proposition in metaphysics will not be one whose conceptual element is entirely pure but rather one containing schematized concepts. And this will, in turn, alter the conception of the way in which Kant seeks to verify such propositions. He does

---

49. Cf. B6, where he says that the concept of substance is more determinate than that of an object in general; also A243 = B301, where he says that the concept of the schema is added to the concept of the pure category of cause. Much of the recent Kant scholarship glosses over what I have called the shift in the chapter on schematism. Having said that the schemata are really supplementary to the categories, Kemp Smith (*op. cit.*, p. 339) goes on to say that "what Kant usually means when he speaks of the categories *are* the schemata." This is true in that Kant usually speaks of the schematized categories, but this leaves it completely undecided how the schemata supplement the categories. Other commentators hold outright that a schema is a concept. Thus Stephan Körner (*Kant* [Baltimore: Penguin Books, 1964], p. 71) says that a schema "is at least the addition of the referential rules of a concept to its non-referential ones. . . ." And Jonathan Bennett (*Kant's Analytic* [Cambridge: Cambridge University Press, 1966], p. 151) says that "a schema seems to be a kind of concept." This, too, is true but leaves it unexplained how Kant relates the pure concepts to the schematized categories. A third view, defended by Gottfried Martin (*Kant's Metaphysics and Theory of Science* [Manchester: Manchester University Press, 1955], p. 84), attempts to explain the relation between a pure and a schematized category by regarding the same concept under two aspects. On Martin's view, for example, "Ontologically regarded, substance is substratum, logically regarded, it is subject." The main exegetical defect of such a view is that, if it were true, it would leave it a mystery why Kant should have ever introduced a chapter on schematism into the *Kritik:* The pure concept alone would be sufficient without being supplemented by any other concept to account for what Kant seeks to explain by the doctrine of schematism.

not, as the traditional account claims, set out to justify the application of concepts to our manifold which have no counterparts in that manifold. The problem about justifying such propositions is rather to show that the objects in our manifold necessarily and universally fall under schematized concepts. But this is a story which must be told later. For the present it is enough to note where the shift in Kant's account of metaphysical propositions takes place.

❦ 4 ❧

Schematism and the Synthetic A Priori

THUS FAR I HAVE TRIED to show that Kant can be held to have given a defensible answer to the question, "How can the right to use a pure concept be established?" only if he is taken to have conceived transcendental schemata as pure intuitions. If I am right, the other theories of transcendental schematism found in Kant are philosophically objectionable. The remaining theory of schematism can now be used to explicate Kant's hidden criterion of syntheticity and, in particular, to explain how, on that theory, there can be any synthetic *a priori* judgments at all. In the following chapter I shall consider two paradigm cases of synthetic *a priori* judgments. Here I want only to state the theory in general and show how the doctrine of schematism is indispensable to it. I shall, however, state the problem in terms of what I have called Kant's hidden criterion. This will not prejudice any issue central to the theory of synthetic *a priori* judgments. It will, in fact, strengthen Kant's position. For I have already argued that, on the explicit theory of syntheticity, there is no reason why every synthetic judgment should not be merely a covert analytic judgment. On the hidden criterion, we at least know why this cannot be so.

What, then, is a synthetic *a priori* judgment on the hidden criterion? The peculiarity of judgments of this kind is that their truth value can be determined independently of experience even though they tell us something about the way the world is. These properties were (and still are) usually thought to be incompatible: Finding the truth value of any proposition which asserts something about the world cannot, it is held, be done without examining particular features of the world. For, so the argument runs, how else can we know whether what the proposition asserts does in fact obtain? Kant's answer to this question, put in the language of his hidden criterion of syntheticity, is as follows. What is asserted by some synthetic judgments can be known independently of experience. Such judgments would assert that a schematized category has a corresponding pure intuition or schema falling under it. We can discover what these schemata are independently of examining particular states of affairs. Yet what is asserted by such judgments holds without exception. And it holds without exception because what we know about the character of pure intuitions cannot be overthrown by any experience, since the character of pure intuition determines the character of any possible experience. This is a preliminary reconstruction of Kant's theory of synthetic judgments *a priori* in metaphysics.[50]

It is important to see that pure intuition is indispensable to this theory. We have already seen that transcendental schemata are pure intuitions. Let us now ask what properties pure intuitions must have in order to function as the schemata of pure concepts. There are two: pure intuitions must be particulars; and they must have instances. I take these properties in turn.

1. Pure intuitions must be particulars. This follows directly from Kant's distinction between intuitions and concepts: "An intuition refers to an object directly and is single. A concept refers to an object

---

50. This was argued in Chapter One. This interpretation of what a synthetic *a priori* proposition is for Kant should distinguish his problem about such propositions from more recent discussions. Cf. esp. Wilfrid Sellars, "Is There a Synthetic *A Priori?*" in Sidney Hook (ed.), *American Philosophers at Work* (New York: Criterion Press, 1958), pp. 135–59 and esp. p. 138, where Sellars puts his question as follows: "Are there any universal propositions which, though they are not logically true, are true by virtue of the meanings of their terms?" But this is very different from the question Kant asks. What Kant wants to know is whether there are any intuitions which can be known to fall under pure concepts. This question has nothing to do with the meaning of a concept but only with whether that concept has a certain kind of intuition falling under it.

indirectly, by means of some respect which may be common to several things." [51] But what is there about an intuition that it must be single? The referent of a singular representation is always an intuition, pure or empirical. Each pure intuition which is singled out is only a part of a single intuition, which is either space or time.[52] But if every pure intuition is only a part of a single all-embracing intuition, then it must be singular, for the single intuition of which it is a part is singular. The same point applies to empirical intuition because pure intuition is a condition of all empirical intuition. Hence transcendental schemata, since they are characteristics of pure intuition, must be particulars. Each pure intuition, then, will fall under the concept of a schematized category because that category is a concept of a characteristic of pure intuition. Both the schemata of permanence in time for substance and succession according to a rule for cause—to take only two examples— are characteristics of pure intuition. They are not characteristics of pure intuitions taken individually; but they are characteristics of pure intuitions as they are related to one another. And these relations will be the particulars which fall under the schematized categories of substance and cause.

2. Pure intuitions must have instances. This must be understood in sharp contrast to the way in which concepts have instantiations. Kant tells us that every concept contains indefinitely many representations *under itself*, while every intuition contains many representations *within itself*.[53] To say that a concept has many instances is to say that many particulars fall under it. Particulars do not fall under other particulars. But this does not prevent particulars from having instances, for the characteristic of one particular can be shared by any particulars which are contained within it. And this is just the result of Kant's argument in the Aesthetic which shows that division performed on space and time does not alter the character of what is divided.[54] Whatever generic characteristics can be established of pure

51. A320 = B377.
52. A24 = B39; cf. *Nachlass*, No. 4315.
53. A25 = B40.
54. A24–25 = B39–40.

intuition will thus be transmitted to any limitation of that intuition. The same point can be put in a different way by saying that, in showing a pure intuition to have a certain feature, one has thereby established that all limitations of that intuition fall under the same concept. It should not be forgotten, however, that there will be generic characteristics of pure intuition which will hold of intuitions separately and others which will hold only of intuitions as they are related to one another.[55] But the principle of intuitional instantiation holds for both of them.

Now intuitions can function as subject terms in synthetic *a priori* judgments. They are expressions for particulars and can therefore be said to refer to what can fall under pure concepts. Moreover, we can know independently of experience that any properties which they exhibit will be instantiated by either all parts or relations of parts of space and time. But another question remains to be answered. Did Kant in fact attribute these two properties to transcendental schemata? I think that he did. That a transcendental schema is a particular follows from my discussion earlier in this chapter. If a transcendental schema is a pure intuition and a pure intuition is a particular, then a transcendental schema is bound to be a particular.

What, then, are the reasons for holding that Kant distinguished between a schema and an instance of a schema? The primary reason for believing that he made such a distinction is that it is implied by what he says about the schema of quantity in the first *Kritik*. Consider, for example, the five dots which Kant says we set down when the number five is counted out. He says this:

> The schema is in itself always a product of imagination. Since, however, the synthesis of imagination aims at no special intuition, but only at unity in the determination of sensibility, the schema has to be distinguished from the image. If five points be set alongside one another, thus, ... , I have an image of the number five. But if, on the other hand, I think only a number in general, whether it be five or a hundred, this thought is rather the representation of a method whereby a multiplicity, for instance a thousand, may be

55. This is the distinction Kant marks when he distinguishes mathematical from dynamical principles (cf. A160–62 = B199–202; A177–80 = B220–23).

represented in an image in conformity with a certain concept, than the image itself.[56]

My only concern with this passage is to give an account of what Kant understands by the distinction between the number five and a picture of the number five. The first thing to notice is that the dots themselves cannot be the schema. At B182 Kant says that *number* is the schema of quantity. The five dots Kant discusses here are not a schema but rather a *picture* of the schema. To find out what Kant could mean by the locution "picture" here, let us compare this passage with what he says at B176. Here he says that part of the task of a schema is to display in intuition the notes or marks which are thought in a concept. This sheds light on what he could have meant by talking about a picture at B179. For a picture is literally an exhibition in intuition. We cannot, however, identify the five dots we draw in intuition with the schema. For Kant says that they are a *picture* as distinct from a schema. But both a schema and a picture would seem to be exhibitions in intuition. How, then, are we to distinguish between the number five and the five dots which Kant calls the picture of a schema? Here there are four things to be related. There are, first, the pure concept of quantity; secondly, the schema of that category; thirdly, the number five; and, fourthly, the image of the number five. Now the schema of the category of quantity is the representation of successive addition. And this does not include the concept of any particular number. So in what way are the five dots an image of the schema? They serve this purpose because they form a picture in intuition which is the result of applying the schema. Now the schema itself is described as a procedure for performing operations in intuition and not as a characteristic of pure intuition. But it should be noted that, when Kant discusses the categories of quantity in the Analytic of Principles, he talks, not about number, but about extensive magnitude.[57] And this *is* a property of all pure intuition as distinct from an operation to be performed on pure intuition: To say that all

56. A140 = B179; cf. A141 = B180.
57. A162 = B202.

intuitions are extensive magnitudes is to claim that they are discrete entities which are measurable.

The apparent discrepancy between number and extensive magnitude can be explained as an example of the twofold function of a schema: it is both a part of the concept specifying a rule of synthesis and a characteristic of the intuition which is synthesized. And this gives us the difference between the image and the schema of quantity. The schema is a characteristic possessed by all intuitions, while the image or picture is a specific instance of that characteristic. The distinction in the case of quantity is just that between being a discrete entity and being a particular number of discrete entities. This shows that Kant does distinguish between transcendental schemata and instances of these schemata.

Let us summarize the foregoing discussion. What I hope to have shown is that Kant's theory of the synthetic *a priori* presupposes his theory of schematism. If we are to be able to form synthetic judgments *a priori*, we must be able to say, independently of examining the infinitely many objects that fall under a concept, that they all have the properties which are combined in the concept. Given Kant's hidden theory of syntheticity, the only way in which we can do this is by discovering the characteristics of pure intuition which are shared either by all intuitions taken separately or by intuitions in relation. This was the problem to which the theory of schematism was meant as a solution. For a transcendental schema has both the characteristics that an object falling under a schematized concept must have: it is a particular and it has instances. Thus the position that there are synthetic judgments *a priori* in metaphysics rests on the position that there are transcendental schemata.

❦ 5 ❧

Objections to the Foregoing Analysis

THE PROCEDURE I FOLLOWED in arriving at my interpretation of Kant's theory of schematism was to find the theory which best satisfied the general requirement Kant lays down for schemata and to regard the other theories which I have distinguished as unsuccessful attempts to satisfy that requirement. Here my concern was a limited one. I was interested only in Kant's theory of transcendental schematism and was content to omit empirical schemata. This way of interpreting schematism is, however, open to a number of objections, all of which consist in the citation of exceptions to the theory I have attributed to Kant. Part of the strength of my interpretation will derive from its power to show that they are not genuine exceptions to the theory I have attributed to Kant.

The first such exception occurs when Kant discusses the schematism of the empirical concept ". . . is a dog." Here he says this:

> The concept "dog" signifies a rule according to which my imagination can delineate the figure of a four-footed animal in a general manner, without limitation to any single determinate figure such as experience, or any possible image that I can represent *in concreto*, actually presents.[58]

The schema of the concept of a dog is not an intuition, as I have suggested, but a figure of a dog-in-general according to which we judge whether particular dogs fall under the concept. But if this is an example of what Kant takes to be an empirical schema, then it is a glaring exception to the view of schematism I have attributed to him. According to this example, Kant apparently wants to distinguish between an intuition and a schema properly so called. The schema will, to be sure, be pictorial; but it will be a rule for constructing a picture of a dog-in-general; hence, it cannot be an intuition.

This example of a schema rests on the assumption that a schema is a third thing which is both general and particular. And I found reason to reject this formulation of schematism as unsatisfactory. Thus what this passage shows is not that Kant would reject the view of a schema as an intuition but that he had other views of schematism as well. And I have not denied this. All I have argued is that we must attribute to Kant the most nearly consistent view we can find which fulfills the requirements laid down for a schema. And to show that there are

58. A141 = B180.

examples listed in Kant's discussion which illustrate one of the other formulations of that theory does not suffice to demonstrate that he did not hold the view I attributed to him.

There is another exception of the same sort which occurs in Kant's discussion of the schema of the pure concept of quantity. Thus he says:

> The pure image of all magnitudes (*quantorum*) for outer sense is space; that of all objects of the senses in general is time. But the pure *schema* of magnitude (*quantitatis*), as a concept of the understanding, is *number*, a representation which comprises the successive addition of homogeneous units.[59]

Here Kant holds that the schema of quantity is number. On the view of schematism that I have attributed to Kant, number would have to be a pure intuition, since quantity is a pure concept. But this view soon runs into difficulties. For one thing, number obviously is not a pure intuition at all. For what property of pure space or pure time could it be? Or, to make matters worse, consider the same questions with respect to the number five. We have already seen how Kant refers to the five dots drawn in space as a picture of the number five. But we surely could not say that every region of space and every span of time had the property of being five merely because we make five dots in pure space. Thus, if we try to work this into the theory of schematism I have offered, we succeed only in extracting nonsense from the text.

The first thing to notice about this apparent exception is that it is introduced by Kant as an illustration of the rule theory of schematism. At B180 he says that the representation of a number is a representation "of a general procedure of the imagination to supply a concept with its picture." Earlier in this chapter I rejected the view that a schema is a rule simply because the view assumed what it was supposed to demonstrate. To say that a schema is a rule for finding an object in intuition assumes that we know there are objects to be found. But this is precisely what the theory of schematism was introduced to prove. What the foregoing example shows is that Kant had a divided

59. A142 = B182.

opinion about what a schema was.[60] But it does not constitute evidence that he rejected the theory I have attributed to him. All I have claimed for my interpretation of his theory of schematism is that it makes sense of what he expects a schema to do and that it accounts for the schemata he actually gives for most of the categories. And the present example does not show that he held the rule theory to the exclusion of the other theories I have distinguished.

The final exception to my interpretation occurs at a point in Kant's discussion of schematism where he says that "the schema of a *pure* concept of understanding can never be brought into any image whatsoever." [61] Earlier in this chapter I used Kant's notion of the picture of a schema to support the view that pure intuitions can be said to have instances. What Kant says here, however, runs counter to the view I have attributed to him. If there is no picture that functions as an instance of the schema of a pure concept, then the distinction made earlier in this chapter between schema and instance of a schema appears to collapse.

The answer to this difficulty can be given by an examination of the context in which Kant denies that the schema of a pure concept can be given an image. Kant calls a transcendental schema the pure synthesis to which the category gives expression. And this is a statement of the rule theory of schematism. If you conceive of a schema as a rule or procedure prescribing the combination of presentations, then it follows that the schema cannot be given an image in either pure or empirical intuition. A procedure can be followed but it cannot be intuited. But this does not constitute an exception to the theory according to which a transcendental schema is a characteristic of pure intuition. For one thing, the rule theory is only one of three theories which can be culled from the chapter on schematism. And for another, it is not incompatible with what I have held to be the dominant theory but rather presupposes that theory.

60. Kant gives another schema for quantity in the Analytic of Principles, where he discusses, not number, but extensive magnitude (cf. A162 = B202).
61. A142 = B181.

§6

Geometrical and Philosophical Reasoning:
A Final Obstacle Removed

ALL METAPHYSICAL PROPOSITIONS which are synthetic express a relation between a schematized category and a pure intuition. To verify such propositions is to show that what is thought in the schematized category has objects falling under it in pure intuition. To show that Kant held both of these propositions is the burden of my account of schematism. But the distinction which Kant makes between geometrical and philosophical reasoning appears to stand in radical opposition to both of these claims. So either the account of schematism at which I have arrived must be seriously modified or the apparent opposition must be removed. I shall take the latter course.

A good statement of the contrast between geometrical and philosophical reasoning is given beginning at A87 = B120; concerning geometry, Kant says that,

grounded as it is in *a priori* intuition, [it] possesses immediate evidence. The objects, so far as their form is concerned, are given, through the very knowledge of them, *a priori* in intuition. In the case of the *pure concepts of the understanding*, it is quite otherwise; it is with them that the unavoidable demand for a transcendental deduction, not only of themselves, but also of the concept of space, first originates. For since they speak of objects through predicates not of intuition and sensibility but of pure *a priori* thought, they relate to objects universally, that is, apart from all conditions of sensibility. Also, not being grounded in experience, they cannot, in *a priori* intuition, exhibit any object such as might, prior to experience, serve as ground of their synthesis.[62]

The opposition to my account of schematism appears plain: no pure concept has any intuition corresponding to it, while a concept in geometry does. Let us contrast the two kinds of reasoning as follows. There are three features distinguishing reasoning in geometry:

62. Cf. A159–60 = B198–99.

1. The concepts of geometry can be exhibited in intuition.[63]
2. Exhibition is accomplished by construction of the relevant figure in pure intuition.[64]
3. Pure intuition supplies images of geometrical concepts from which characteristics belonging to all objects falling under the concept can be read off.[65]

Contrast this with the way in which Kant characterizes reasoning in philosophy:

1. The pure categories are not concepts of a specific kind of object but of an object in general.[66]
2. "For the concept of a *thing* in general . . . no intuition can be given *a priori*." [67]
3. Propositions in philosophy are established by showing that they are conditions of the synthesis of particular objects which are given in intuition.[68]

The conclusion to which this contrast gives rise is that "a transcendental proposition . . . gives no intuition *a priori*." [69] And yet this conclusion cannot be used to show that propositions in philosophy are established without reference to pure intuition. The first thing to notice about this contrast is that Kant sets apart *pure concepts* from those in geometry. It is true that there is no intuition corresponding to pure concepts, not because philosophical proof dispenses with pure intuition, but only because what counts as a pure concept is discovered independently of intuition.

The second thing to notice about the contrast is that it concerns the way in which concepts are constructed. A geometer is said to construct his basic concepts by reference to the properties of intuition. A philosopher cannot do this. For what corresponds in philosophy to the basic

63. A159 = B198.
64. A713 = B741.
65. A713–14 = B741–42.
66. A251 = B307.
67. A720 = B748.
68. *Ibid.*
69. A722 = B750.

concepts of the geometer is the list of pure concepts which form the basis of metaphysics. And a list of such concepts cannot be drafted by reading off properties of intuition because, as we have seen, pure concepts refer to a manifold in general and are thus compatible with the characteristics any manifold might have.

The contrast is, then, quite neutral about whether concepts in philosophy must have *a priori* intuitions corresponding to them. All that is being described here is a difference in the procedure of discovering basic concepts. The discovery of schemata is not mentioned; hence, the contrast holds only between two ways of constructing basic concepts and investigating their implications. Nor do other statements Kant makes about transcendental propositions constitute an exception to this conclusion. He says that transcendental propositions give no intuition *a priori;* and he even says that transcendental propositions "have no third factor, that is to say, no object, in which the synthetic unity of their concepts can be shown to have objective validity." [70] The reason that transcendental propositions give no intuition *a priori* is that the concepts in such propositions are pure. And to say that such propositions have no object in which their synthesis can be shown to have objective validity is also understandable: They give the rules of synthesis for an object in general. And they accordingly can be shown to make experience of objects possible once it is demonstrated that they are conditions of our thought of an object in general.

But none of this removes the requirement Kant makes that the pure concepts be schematized before they can be shown to be the conditions of synthesizing objects in our manifold. And he states this requirement repeatedly:

No synthetic proposition can be made from categories alone . . . that is, where there is nothing that could enable us to go beyond a given concept and connect another concept with it. . . . In order to demonstrate the *objective reality* of the categories, we require intuitions.[71]

70. A157 = B196.
71. A235 = B289. Cf. Kant's letter to Reinhold (*Werke*, IX, 402) and his reply to Eberhard (*Werke*, VI, 62).

Beginning at A240 = B299 Kant first lays down the condition that "a bare concept be *made sensible,* that is, that an object corresponding to it be presented in intuition." He then goes on to demand this of concepts in mathematics; and, more importantly, he extends the same requirement to cover philosophical concepts by saying that, "if this connection be removed, all meaning, that is, relation to the object, falls away; and we cannot through any example make comprehensible to ourselves what sort of a thing is to be meant by such a concept." [72]

We must, however, be cautious about the interpretation of these passages. Kant does demand that concepts in philosophy, like those in geometry, be related to intuition. But the intuition which he demands might be merely empirical and not *a priori* intuition. An unrelenting advocate of the interpretation according to which there is no intuition which specifically corresponds to pure concepts could argue that pure concepts are related to intuitions when those concepts are shown to be the rules governing our combination of empirical intuitions. And this, it might be argued, does not require that a pure intuition correspond to anything thought in the pure concept.

That such an interpretation is possible is the result of the shift in Kant's argument in the chapter on schematism which I have already noted. That shift occurs when he transfers his attention from pure categories to schematized categories. The former gives us rules for combining a manifold to form an object. And a large part of Kant's argument preceding the chapter on schematism is directed at showing that pure concepts do apply to empirical intuitions. But then there is a change in the concepts which are taken to apply to intuitions. Pure concepts are schematized; and it is these concepts, not the pure concepts which are identified in the Metaphysical Deduction, that figure in the synthetic *a priori* propositions of metaphysics. And so, the

---

72. Cf. A155–56 = B194–95; but esp. B73: "When in *a priori* judgment we seek to go out beyond the given concept, we come in the *a priori* intuitions upon that which cannot be discovered in the concept but which is certainly found *a priori* in the intuition corresponding to the concept, and can be connected with it synthetically."

reason that the present interpretation of these passages is not admissible is that it overlooks the results of the doctrine of schematism: a schematized category, unlike a pure category, must contain a concept which does refer to features of pure intuition. That there are good philosophical as well as exegetical reasons for recognizing the shift of attention which takes place in the chapter on schematism was the burden of section 5 of the present chapter.

⟨7⟩
Concluding Remarks

IT HAS BEEN MY PURPOSE here to show why the chapter on schematism should have been put into the *Kritik* in the first place by arguing that the problem of schematism is part of the problem of synthetic *a priori* judgments. A recognition of this, apart from the help it gives us in evaluating Kant's theory of the *a priori*, has the advantage of enabling us to see the point of the question with which Kant begins the chapter on schematism.[73] There, it will be remembered, he asks how pure concepts can be applied to phenomena. The problem this set us was this: It was not immediately clear why Kant would want to ask the question he does in this way, since it is far from clear how the introduction of further entities called schemata could help in answering it. My solution to this problem was to show that Kant offers, not one, but three formulations of the theory of schematism. Only one of these theories succeeded in explaining how categories can be applied to phenomena and, further, why schemata must be different from both concepts and the phenomena to which they are applied.

Why, then, *does* Kant ask how categories can be applied to phenomena? We are now in a position to understand this, for we can now see that the question Kant asks is not one question but two. One of his concerns is to find referents for pure concepts. The structural motive for asking this question is Kant's theory of meaning, according to which a category is given meaning or objective validity when its

73. A138 = B177.

referent can be exhibited in intuition. But there is also the different, but not unrelated, task of showing how the categories can apply to phenomena. How, that is, are we justified in saying that all appearances must fall under the categories?

These are, of course, two quite distinct questions. And it is not inconceivable that Kant could have answered one (What are the referents of pure concepts?) without having answered the other (How can we prove claims that the categories apply without exception to all phenomena?). The importance of the chapter on schematism is to show that for Kant an answer to the first question would also be an answer to the second. For if the referents of schematized concepts are, as Kant holds, pure intuitions, then Kant has succeeded in explaining both what the referents of categories are and how appearances must fall under the categories. These questions are, however, obscured in the introduction to the chapter on schematism, where he asks merely how subsumption of appearances under categories is possible. If my interpretation of schematism is correct, what Kant is asking there are two quite distinct questions. That they are not unrelated is the structural key to the significance of schematism for the first *Kritik* and, hence, to an understanding of Kant's solution to the problem of the synthetic *a priori*.

CHAPTER FIVE

Schematism and

the Analogies

S O FAR I HAVE BEEN ARGUING for two claims: that Kant's arguments in both the Analytic and the Dialectic assume a theory of syntheticity according to which an intuition is related to a concept; and that the theory of schematism in the first *Kritik* is a theory about the relation of intuitions and concepts in synthetic judgments. Now I should like to use the results of these arguments to assess the first and second Analogies of Experience. My assessment will consist in unraveling a badly snarled set of problems surrounding the first two Analogies. By doing this, however, we shall see whether Kant can show that there are really any synthetic *a priori* judgments in metaphysics.

The first problem is to understand why the Analogies should be synthetic propositions at all. The characteristics which Kant assigns to the Analogies on the explicit theory of the synthetic-analytic distinction are compatible with the analyticity of both the propositions stating the Analogies. At no time did Kant entertain the possibility that these propositions could be anything but synthetic. Yet, given the distinction between synthetic and analytic propositions as he sets it out, there is no structural reason why he should have thought this. My purpose here will be to supply those reasons by examining the first two Analogies in terms of what I have called the hidden criterion of syntheticity.

I pass then to the second problem about the Analogies. This concerns Kant's specific arguments for them. Two questions are relevant here. On the criterion of syntheticity implicit in Kant's arguments, the only way in which he can establish a synthetic *a priori* proposition is by exhibiting in pure intuition a particular which falls under the pure concept whose applicability he wants to establish. Whether this can in fact be done by the arguments Kant gives for the first two Analogies will constitute the first question. But what if this cannot be done by Kant's arguments? If no such intuition can be exhibited, then what do the arguments for the first two Analogies establish? This will constitute the second question.

There remains, however, another problem. How do the arguments which Kant offers for both the first and the second Analogy illustrate the transcendental method of proof? The results of the preceding discussion will be used here to show that the difficulty in interpreting what the transcendental method is can be traced to the difficulty of arriving at a straight account of what the Kantian synthetic-analytic distinction is. Here it will be important to show that the method of proof involved in the transcendental method differs according to the way you interpret the synthetic-analytic distinction. But what is even more important is to see that on neither interpretation of that distinction discussed in Chapter Two does Kant give us an effective way of separating propositions which state the conclusions of a transcendental argument from those which do not.

I am aware that I am restricting my analysis of the synthetic *a priori* in metaphysics to only two of the examples which Kant gives in the first *Kritik*. But there is good reason for doing this. I am omitting consideration of the Axioms of Intuitions and the Anticipation of Perception because Kant gives only the principle which can be used to generate specific synthetic *a priori* propositions; he thus does not give examples of such propositions generated from the principle. Neither one of these sections of the Analytic can be used as a test case for the hidden theory of syntheticity. In this respect, however, the third Analogy of Experience is different. It does give us an example of a synthetic *a priori* proposition. But an understanding of Kant's procedure in the first and second Analogies will permit ready extension to the third.

There are, finally, the Postulates of Empirical Thought. They purport to be synthetic and *a priori*. But Kant's statement of the Postulates has the appearance of definition which neither the manifest nor the implicit theories of syntheticity can remove.[1] To say, for example, that what agrees with the formal conditions of experience is possible may be a metaphysical proposition; but it is one that is ineradicably analytic. Such a proposition merely tells us what lies in the concept of experiential possibility. It does not tell is that there are any objects which fall under that concept. And the concept of agreement with the formal conditions of experience is clearly part of the concept of possibility as it is used here. This is also true of the concepts of actuality and necessity. To say that what is bound up with the material conditions of experience is actual can only be an analytic proposition. For what else would be the analysis of actuality as Kant uses the concept here? What follows as the third Postulate is also an analytic proposition. If anything is determined in accordance with universal conditions of experience, this makes it necessary. And this is an analysis of the notion of necessity. Kant perhaps recognized this, although he nowhere explicitly claims that the Postulates are analytic, when he gives us, not a *proof*, but an *explanation* of the Postulates.[2] The former concept applies to propositions which cannot be shown to be true by inspecting the concepts which constitute them. Thus they

1. A218 = B266.
2. *Ibid.*

require a justification or deduction which, on Kant's view, can only be given by a transcendental proof. The latter concept would, accordingly, be applied to those propositions for which no such proof is necessary; and since the propositions expressing the Postulates are not synthetic *a posteriori*, the only other way in which they could be shown to be true would be through the Law of Contradiction—which would assume that the propositions in question are analytic; hence, Kant could be expected to call his discussion of these propositions an explanation rather than a proof. These propositions are, in any case, patently analytic; hence I shall not consider them here.

This is not the only restriction which I shall place on my discussion of Kant's examples of metaphysical propositions. Here I want only to ask in what way the propositions formulating the first and second Analogies can be construed as synthetic and *a priori*, following this by asking whether the arguments Kant gives are sufficient to establish them when they are construed in this way. I shall not ask whether such notions as permanence in time or necessary succession according to a rule can withstand objections to their philosophical adequacy.

The Syntheticity of the First Analogy

WHAT, THEN, ARE THE REASONS for supposing that the first and second Analogies do in fact express propositions which are synthetic and *a priori*? First let us see how Kant states the first Analogy. He gives two different statements of it. The first statement is this: "All appearances contain the permanent (substance) as the object itself, and the transitory as its mere determination, that is, as a way in which the object exists." [3] The second statement runs as follows: "In all change of appearances substance is permanent; its *quantum* in nature is neither increased nor diminished." [4]

These two formulations are, of course, quite different. The first is a

3. A182.
4. A224.

statement about continuants in experience. The second is a statement about the conservation of matter within a system. For it states that the quantity of matter within a system is constant. And this is different from saying, as the first formulation does, that the quantity of matter in any object within that system is constant. The first formulation is a statement about the character of the system as a whole, while the second is a statement about the character of objects within that system. And they are not logically equivalent. You could, for example, hold that the quantity of matter within a *system* is constant and still deny that it is constant for any *object* within that system. I therefore do not propose to discuss the second formulation at all but will rather take the first as the stronger version of Kant's view. The reason for this is simple: The arguments for the first Analogy prove, if they establish anything at all, something about continuants in nature. They are quite silent about the conservation of matter.

The first thing to notice about the first Analogy is that the explicit formulation of the synthetic-analytic distinction is powerless to explain why it is synthetic rather than analytic. In order to show this, let us first identify the subject and predicate concepts in the formulation in the A edition of the *Kritik*. The subject—as distinct from the subject *concept*—of the judgment is the totality of appearances. The concept of the subject is "appearance" while the predicate concept here is ". . . contains the permanent (substance) as the object itself and the transitory as its mere determination." One way of explaining why the first Analogy is synthetic is to point out that the concept of an appearance does not contain the concept of containing anything that is permanent: We can conceive of appearances that did not contain the permanent at all.

But this defense of the syntheticity of the first Analogy loses its plausibility once it is seen that, while an existent can be conceived that is not permanent, the same need not hold for an appearance. And Kant himself gives us a good reason for thinking that the same does not hold for an appearance when he says that "all our representations are, it is true, referred to some object; and since appearances are nothing but representations, the understanding refers them to a something, as the object of sensible intuition." [5] An appearance is thus just that which betokens the existence of an object. And this is reason for thinking that the predicate of the first Analogy is included in the concept of the subject.

Another reason for coming to the same conclusion is that, since the first Analogy is *a priori*, the connection between the referents of the two concepts is universal and necessary. It is universal in that there is no exception to what such propositions assert; necessary, in that they have inconceivable denials. But both of these requirements are satisfied by analytic propositions. And if we assume that the first Analogy meets them, why have we not been given a sufficient reason for holding that it is analytic?

One way of answering these questions runs as follows. According to the remarks with which Kant introduces the Analytic of Principles, what makes the first Analogy synthetic is the relation it has to intuition.

> Synthetic *a priori* judgments are thus possible when we relate the formal conditions of *a priori* intuition, the synthesis of imagination and the necessary unity of this synthesis in a transcendental apperception, to a possible empirical knowledge in general. We then assert that the conditions of the *possibility of experience* in general are likewise conditions of the *possibility of objects of experience*, and that for this reason they have objective validity in a synthetic *a priori* judgment.[6]

What we are told here comes to this. The first Analogy cannot be analytic for Kant since it tells us something which is a condition of experience. It tells us something about appearances. And we cannot discover this by analyzing the concept of appearance but only by establishing the applicability to experience of such concepts as substance. The first Analogy is a statement about appearances, not about "appearance."

But this way of answering our questions is not satisfactory. For

---

5. A250; cf. A249. Kant sometimes thinks that the formulation of the first Analogy given in B is analytic. In *Nachlass*, No. 6403, he says: "In every change the substance continues. . . . This is a purely logical proposition."
6. A158 = B197.

what we are asking when we inquire whether the first Analogy is synthetic or analytic is whether the predicate which is asserted in the first Analogy is or is not contained in the subject concept. We are not asking anything about the relation of the proposition to the world. What Kant says in the above quotation cannot, therefore, be taken as a satisfactory reply to our questions. For it is, strictly speaking, irrelevant to them. The question about what is or is not thought in a concept is not settled by pointing out that propositions which are synthetic tell us something about the world. For this tells us only about the relation of the proposition to the world and not about the relation of concepts within the proposition. For all we learn from this kind of answer, the first Analogy might very well be analytic. Thus the explicit theory of syntheticity, far from illuminating the problem that Kant has with synthetic *a priori* propositions, is unable to explain why Kant ever did think that the first Analogy was synthetic.

Consider the first Analogy interpreted according to the hidden criterion of syntheticity. The expression for the subject would then refer to particulars. The predicate expression would stand for a concept. The latter is not hard to identify: it is the schematized concept of substance. But is there an expression in Kant's formulation of the first Analogy that refers to intuitions? Here "appearances" serves as such an expression. Yet it is indeterminate as to what kinds of appearances, pure or empirical, it is meant to denote. This can, however, be decided indirectly by asking the kinds of objects to which the predicate applies. The permanent in time, Kant tells us, is really time itself as the permanent form of inner intuition.[7] But this means that the predicate of the first Analogy refers to a characteristic of pure intuition. Thus the subject of the proposition is the pure intuition of time and, derivatively, empirical intuitions which the former makes possible. The proposition asserts, then, that there are objects which fall under the schematized concept of substance. And these objects are characteristics of pure intuition.

This interpretation of the first Analogy makes it a synthetic propo-

7. B224.

sition. It is also an *a priori* proposition. This, too, can be explained by the implicit theory of judgment. Such a proposition, if it is true at all, would be necessarily and universally true. It would tell us something about experience to which there is no exception. And this is exactly what the first Analogy, interpreted as a claim about the instantiation of the schematized concept of substance, would do. The objects instantiating the concept are characteristics of pure intuition. Since pure intuition defines the form of our sensibility, whatever characteristics pure intuition can be shown to have will hold without exception for any experience given to that sensibility.

☙ 2 ❧

Schematism and the Hidden Criterion
of Syntheticity

THE HIDDEN CRITERION CAN, therefore, explain why the first Analogy expresses a synthetic proposition. One of the requirements of the implicit criterion of syntheticity when it is applied to the first Analogy is that there be a pure intuition which corresponds to the pure concept of substance. Is there such an intuition? I have already argued that, if there is such an intuition, it must be pure and that, secondly, such a pure intuition would be the transcendental schema of the concept. But there are difficulties with this view when we try to analyze the first Analogy in terms of it. Kant says that time itself is the schema of substance.[8] Yet, this alone cannot be the theory Kant holds because he elsewhere denies that we can perceive time itself. What we perceive is, not time itself, but temporal relations.

But the schema Kant gives in place of time itself entirely fails as a schema. Kant infers from our inability to perceive time itself that the only adequate schema of substance is the permanent in time.[9] This alternative is inadequate. For permanence in time is not a property of time at all. It refers to something that goes on in time; and this is

8. A143 = B183.
9. Cf. A181–82 = B224–25.

quite different from time itself. On Kant's theory of transcendental schematism, the only characteristics of experience about which we can have information independently of experience are pure space and pure time. Permanence in time is neither of these. So even if the permanent in time could function as the schema of substance, we could not, on Kant's theory, be able to know this independently of experience. The judgment that substance has as its schema the permanent in time could not, therefore, express a synthetic *a priori* proposition. Our examination of the first Analogy leaves us, then, with the following uncomfortable alternative. If we interpret the first Analogy in terms of the criterion of syntheticity which Kant says he uses, then we have no good reason at all for thinking it to express a synthetic proposition. But if we seek to interpret the first Analogy in accordance with Kant's hidden criterion of syntheticity, the first Analogy cannot express a synthetic proposition that is *a priori*.

There is, however, an interpretation of Kant's argument for the first Analogy that might enable him to show how permanence in time is really a property of time itself which is then transferred to any object in time. The interpretation runs like this. What is permanent cannot change, although what is related to it can. Time is permanent in this way since it is a substratum within which all change takes place. Time itself cannot change. And what does change must do so in time. But since permanence is a characteristic of time, it will be a characteristic of whatever occurs within time, since the characteristics of pure intuition are inherited by whatever is contained within it.

This reconstruction of Kant's argument is, however, unsuccessful. To say that time is permanent through change is not to say that whatever is *in* time is permanent through change. You can consistently hold that time is permanent through change and that whatever is in time is instantaneous. It is true that the permanence which is attributed to time itself is also a characteristic which every part of time has. But this is precisely what renders time itself incapable of giving us the schema of substance. Each part of time is permanent; and this is compatible with there being nothing that endures through time. To say that time itself is permanent commits you to saying only that every part of time is permanent—that it does not change. And this is compatible with denying that there is anything else in time that endures through those time spans that is permanent. Hence the reconstruction does not give Kant's argument the conclusion it must have if he is to prove that there are substances in time.

The conclusion to which we have been forced by an examination of Kant's hidden criterion of judgment should not be used to show that Kant did not, after all, employ such a criterion in the first Analogy. Kant sets out to prove that there are permanent objects through time. And it should be remembered that, on the criterion of synthetic judgment that he professes to employ, it is unclear why he should have thought that the proposition he was trying to prove was synthetic at all. What is illuminating about seeing the proof he offers in the context of the covert theory of synthetic judgment is that we can understand the root of the difficulty with his argument. The difficulty with the argument is, as I have been trying to point out, with the compatibility of instantaneousness with permanence. The concept that Kant undertakes to apply to experience here is that of permanence through time. The relation which he chooses to employ as the experiential counterpart of this concept is that between time itself and moments in time. There is, as I have argued, a difficulty with this move that vitiates the argument as it stands: The sense in which continuants through time are permanent is very different from the sense in which time is permanent. Time itself is permanent in that it cannot occupy places in the time series. Individual continuants through time are permanent in that they are numerically identical although they do occupy different positions in the time series. This is why the schema which Kant offers is not adequate to the concept of a continuant through time. But attention to the covert criterion of syntheticity at work in this argument explains why Kant should have tried to equate the sense in which time itself is permanent with the sense in which continuants through time are permanent. Kant has set himself the task of showing that a category has something corresponding to it in pure intuition. And that pure intuition is too impoverished to instantiate the concept Kant wants to instantiate does not show the absence of the covert theory of syntheticity in the argument. It shows only that the covert theory makes demands on pure intuition which it cannot fulfill. At least we are given a reason why Kant should have wanted to make those demands on pure intuition in the first place. That is what is illuminating about the presence of the covert theory in the argument for the first Analogy.

⟨3⟩

The Syntheticity of the Second Analogy

FINDING A SCHEMA for causality leads to similar, but not identical, difficulties. Kant's statement of the second Analogy does not vary in any important way from the first to the second edition of the *Kritik*. The second-edition statement differs from that of the first edition only in that it mentions what the first-edition account states, which is the following: "Everything that happens, that is, begins to be, presupposes something upon which it follows according to a rule." [10] Here we are given a property of pure intuition as a schema (succession of points in the time series). All that is required for schematizing the pure concept of causality is to establish that, for any point on the time series, there is a point prior to it. It would accordingly appear that the schema of causality signalizes at least one property of objects which we can know independently of experience and hence that the proposition stating the applicability of the concept to pure intuition is a genuine synthetic *a priori* proposition.

But a little reflection will show that temporal succession is not enough to schematize the concept of causality. Kant wants to distinguish between a properly causal sequence and what he calls subjective time order. For every order in which I perceive events is not a causal order. Kant shows this when he cites the example of the way in which we are presented with a complex object like a house:

10. A189.

For instance, the apprehension of the manifold in the appearance of a house which stands before me is successive. The question then arises, whether the manifold of the house is also in itself successive.[11]

When we go around a house, we are presented with a different series of parts depending upon how we choose to circle the house. This is an example which Kant uses to prove the successive character of our perception of any manifold. And it is also an example he uses to show that successive presentation of a manifold as such is inadequate to schematize the pure concept of causality. If the only property of pure time required to schematize causality were succession, then we could not distinguish between *causal* succession and the kind of succession which every manifold has.

It is not, however, clear that we can find any property of pure time which would enable us to distinguish between these two kinds of succession. Suppose we follow Kant in making the schema of causality, not merely temporal succession, but objective succession in time. Then we will, to be sure, have schematized the concept of causality. And we will have succeeded in distinguishing between any temporal sequence and the kind of temporal sequence which is properly causal. But then other difficulties break out. The distinction between objective and subjective time orders cannot be made *a priori*. That is, what Kant calls the objective time order cannot be shown to be a property of pure time. We can know independently of experience that the parts of the time series are necessarily succeeded by other parts. This is only another way of saying that there is no part of time for which we cannot supply an antecedent point in time.[12] But this is not all we mean by speaking of an objective time order. The property I have just mentioned belongs to any time series, objective or subjective. It will not suffice to distinguish one kind of time order from another.

To bring this out more clearly, consider how Kant proposes to distinguish between the two time orders. He points out that what we

11. A190 = B235.
12. This is brought out clearly in Kant's discussion of the second Antinomy, A438–43 = B466–71.

ordinarily consider to be a perceptual object is given to us in a series of presentations:

> The apprehension of the manifold of appearance is always successive. The representations of the parts follow upon one another. Whether they also follow one another in the object is a point which calls for further reflection, and which is not decided by the above statement.[13]

More specifically, whenever I perceive an object:

> I am conscious only that my imagination sets the one state before and the other after, not that the one state precedes the other in the object. In other words, the *objective relation* of appearances that follow upon one another is not to be determined through mere perception.[14]

The example Kant gives of this is the ship whose movement downstream is irreversible:

> I see a ship move downstream. My perception of its lower position follows upon the perception of its position higher in the stream, and it is impossible that in the apprehension of this appearance the ship should first be perceived lower down in the stream and afterwards higher up. The order in which the perceptions succeed one another in apprehension is in this instance determined, and to this order apprehension is bound down.[15]

The movement of the ship downstream takes place successively. The distinction between an objective and a subjective time order consists in the irreversibility of the latter. If the ship's movement downstream were a case of subjective time order, we should be able to reverse the order in which the manifold is presented to us.

The distinction Kant makes between a subjective and an objective time order comes to this. The time order in which the manifold is presented is subjective if I can vary it at will. This is illustrated by the example of our apprehension of the house, where we can govern the sequence in which we apprehend it. There are other sequences, like that of the ship's movement downstream, which we allegedly cannot vary. And the order in which such a manifold is presented is for Kant objective.

13. A189 = B234.
14. B233–34.
15. A192 = B237.

This way of making the distinction between time orders gives us irreversibility as the property of pure intuition which schematizes the pure concept of causality. It can, however, be shown that the property of irreversibility belongs to both subjective and objective time orders. Consider the sense in which the movement of the ship downstream is irreversible. Having perceived the ship first at a point upstream and later at another point downstream, I cannot, according to Kant, perceive the positions reversed. But this is less a fact about an objective as distinct from a subjective time series than it is a fact about both indifferently. To see this, consider the house example. If I synthesize first part *P* and then part *Q*, there is a sense in which I cannot reverse this sequence. Events which are located at past points in the time series cannot be changed. So there is one sense in which the manifold of a house is just as irreversible as the manifold of a moving ship. Each manifold consists of preceding and succeeding parts which cannot be reversed because they have unique positions in the time series. The manifold of the ship moving downstream is irreversible only in this sense. It is not irreversible in the sense that I am unable to picture the ship first downstream and then upstream. But if it is not irreversible in this latter sense, then the only other sense in which it could be irreversible is the sense in which *every* manifold is irreversible. And this will not give us a distinction between subjective and objective time sequences.

There is an obvious objection to the foregoing argument. It runs as follows. The reason that the manifold of the ship is different from the manifold by which I apprehend a house is that, in the former, I cannot first see the ship upstream, then downstream, and then upstream again. When I synthesize the manifold of a house, however, I can see the top, a side, and then transfer my attention to the top again. Thus, although each presentation does indeed occupy a unique position in the time series, we can, according to this objection, still distinguish between two kinds of time order in terms of irreversibility. I can alter the manifold of a house in a way that I cannot change that of a moving ship. The latter is irreversible in a way that the former is not.

This way of arguing for the distinction between time orders is a failure. What it points out is factually correct; but the conclusion drawn from this is unsound. It is true that we cannot move from seeing a ship at position P_1 to seeing it at P_2 and then move to seeing it at P_1 again. And we cannot do this simply because moving ships are not stationary. Houses, being stationary, permit the observer more freedom in directing his attention to the parts composing them. But these are not facts about a time series, subjective or objective. They are commonplaces about the course that a moving ship takes and what makes moving ships different from objects which do not move.[16] What makes the manifold of a house different from that of a moving ship has nothing to do with the property that an objective time series must have. That I can move around a house in varying ways does not show the sequence of representations that results from this movement to be any less objective than the sequence which results from the movement of a ship downstream. It is just as much an objective property of the house that it presents itself in a certain way to different perspectives as it is an objective property of the ship that it presents itself to an observer in a certain sequence. My conclusion is that irreversibility has not been shown to be a property of an objective

16. Graham Bird (*Kant's Theory of Knowledge* [New York: Humanities Press, 1962], p. 155) attempts to show how the ship example does illustrate the distinction between objective and subjective time orders as follows: "The necessity in such a case is the logical necessity that to apprehend a ship's sailing downstream is, necessarily, to apprehend an event in which the ship's position downstream followed its position upstream. The order of *this* event is a necessary order, not because it is impossible for ships to sail upstream, but because if the constituent states had been reversed the event apprehended would have been a different event. It would have been the event of a ship's sailing upstream." If this is Kant's argument, the conclusion I have drawn in the text finds additional support. For this argument can equally well be used to prove that the order in which I perceive the manifold of a house is objective simply because to have perceived it in another order would be to have perceived another event. This consequence is, however, prima facie evidence that Bird's reconstruction would not have been welcomed by Kant. The same argument could, for example, be used to show the objectivity of the sequence in which the observer brings together the manifold composed of the sides of a house. And this would, in turn, obliterate the distinction Kant seeks to make between the manifold of a house and the manifold of a moving ship.

as opposed to a subjective time series. For no distinction has been given to set apart the two types of temporal succession.

This has a serious consequence for Kant's attempt to schematize the concept of causality. If objective sequence in time is the schema of causality, then Kant will, to be sure, have pointed out a property of pure time which falls under the concept of causality. But objective sequence is explicated in terms of irreversibility, which is a characteristic of both subjective and objective time sequences alike. Thus, while irreversibility is a property of pure intuition, it is not a property that will distinguish an objective from a subjective temporal sequence. The schema which Kant gives us for causality is, then, inadequate. But if the schema is inadequate, then the second Analogy, although it expresses a synthetic *a priori* proposition, will express a synthetic *a priori* proposition that is false.

ᘚ4ᘛ
Opposing Interpretations

H. J. PATON IS UNCONVINCED by the foregoing attack on irreversibility. He says:

Kant is not arguing from the observed irreversibility of my sense-perceptions to an objective succession. He is on the contrary arguing from an assumed objective succession to the irreversibility of my sense-perceptions. He is not saying that I find I cannot reverse the order of my sense-perceptions, and then conclude I must be dealing with an objective succession. . . . Kant starts with the assumption that we are aware of an objective succession, and asserts that, if so, our sense perceptions must occur in a particular order.[17]

Paton denies part of the foundation on which my criticism of Kant rests. We do not, according to Paton, observe irreversibility in a temporal sequence. On Paton's account, Kant begins with the observation of objective succession and then argues back to irreversibility as a

17. H. J. Paton, *Kant's Metaphysic of Experience* (2 vols.; London: George Allen & Unwin, 1951), II, 239.

condition without which we could not observe objective succession.

But this interpretation of Kant's argument does not render my criticism invalid. This can be seen by paying attention to the notion of objective succession. For Kant it means "independence of the order of an observer's apprehension." This means merely that I am unable to arrange the manifold differently. So "irreversibility" and "objective succession" are synonyms. To assert the one is to assert the other. It is strange, therefore, that Paton should think that Kant wants to *argue* from the one to the other. Even if Kant did start by assuming objective succession while intending to argue to the conclusion that such a succession was irreversible, his procedure in the proof for the second Analogy would be question-begging. For what, on Paton's account, Kant assumes simply cannot be assumed on Kant's premises. The question Kant is asking is whether we can know that there is any such thing as objective succession in the manifold. Kant does not begin by assuming such an order since the existence of such an order is what is in question.

I suppose that Paton would disagree with this from what he says later:

> We can recognize the subjective only when we distinguish it from the objective (this is Kant's own view); for "subjective" and "objective" are correlative terms which mean nothing except in relation to each other. And if we started with awareness of something merely subjective, it would, so far as I can see, be impossible to pass to knowledge of the objective.[18]

This position, which Paton rightly rejects, must be strictly distinguished from the one I have held above. The problem for Kant is how we can recognize whether any sequence is subjective or objective. But this does not commit me to saying that we start from an avowedly subjective sequence and only then move to an objective sequence. We do not *infer* objective sequences from subjective ones; we *distinguish* them from each other.

The attempt to schematize the category of cause remains where it was before. The schema for that category is necessary succession ac-

18. *Ibid.*, p. 272.

cording to a rule. This in turn is translated into a transcendental determination of time as irreversibility. But what is wrong with irreversibility of temporal succession is that we cannot distinguish, as Kant wants to do, between a kind of succession which is not causal and one which Kant wants to recognize as causal. This is not an objection to irreversibility as a mark of a causal sequence. But it is an objection to irreversibility as a characteristic of pure intuition in virtue of which a causal sequence is to be distinguished from one which is not. Thus the attempt to schematize both substance and causality breaks down. The schema of substance—the permanent in time—is adequate as an example of substance. But the permanent in time is not a property of pure intuition. The assertion that the permanent in time falls under the concept of substance cannot be synthetic *a priori*. The schema of causality—objective temporal succession—is, unlike the schema of substance, a property of pure intuition. But it is a property shared alike by subjective and objective succession. So the assertion that objective temporal succession falls under the concept of causality is false because it is an inadequate schema of causality.

⟨5⟩

The Second Analogy and the Manifest Theory of Judgment

NECESSARY SUCCESSION according to a rule cannot be given a schema that is a relation in pure intuition. There is no pure intuition which falls under that concept; and thus the second Analogy does not express a true proposition that is synthetic and *a priori*. What must be considered at this point is whether the manifest theory of judgment present in the *Kritik* can yield a synthetic *a priori* proposition when it is applied to the second Analogy. The subject of the second Analogy is alterations; hence, the subject concept is that of alteration. And the predicate in the proposition is ". . . presupposes something upon which it follows according to a rule." The subject concept of this proposition will not, so the theory goes, yield the predicate upon analysis. We can readily conceive of an alteration whose parts are not causally related. Every manifold is successive. And this alone counts as alteration. But the mere presence of succession in the manifold is exhibited when, for example, we move around a stationary object. This is not causal. Thus the proposition expressing a relation between alteration and necessary succession according to a rule is synthetic.

The difficulty with this account of the second Analogy is that it cannot explain why Kant should ever have thought that proposition to be synthetic. Let us assume that our apprehension of every manifold is successive. The question is whether every such apprehension is a genuine case of alteration. It is a genuine experience of happening or occurrence. We may not infer that it is therefore an experience of alteration. What this proves is that what is at issue is the appropriate designation of the succession which for Kant characterizes every manifold. That other characterizations are possible which do justice to this quality of the manifold but do not force us to use the same concept as the one which we employ in connection with causal succession shows that the concept of causal sequence can be contained in the concept of alteration. The manifest theory of judgment leaves us with a mystery which is unsolved by an examination of Kant's argument for the second Analogy. We are asked to assume that the subject expression of the second Analogy refers to things which can conceivably be causally unrelated to one another. Such an expression would, accordingly, refer to the events which occur successively in our apprehension of the manifold. And it is apparently about these events that Kant is talking when he seeks to prove that all alteration presupposes something upon which it follows according to a rule. But Kant holds that there are some successive sequences which are not causally related.

And this generates the mystery. How could Kant hold both that there are sequences of events which are not causally related while holding that the subject expression of the second Analogy refers indifferently to all cases of succession? The answer is that he cannot hold both views. If the subject expression of the second Analogy refers to all cases of succession, then Kant cannot prove that they are causally related to one another. But if the subject concept of the second Analogy refers, not to all cases of succession, but only to sequences that are causally related, then the second Analogy will have been transformed into an analytic proposition. What is wrong here, I suggest, is the conception of what a synthetic proposition must be. As long as we look upon a synthetic proposition for Kant as a relation between two concepts, the mystery that I have just sketched will remain. If we adopt the implicit theory of judgment, we can explain why Kant should have thought the second Analogy to be synthetic rather than analytic.

There have been two ways in which Kant scholars have sought to show that the second Analogy is synthetic. Both of them tacitly assume that the proposition as interpreted according to the manifest theory is synthetic and seek to show that the proposition is true by reference to the arguments Kant gives for it. The first account of the argument runs like this. Kant assumes the existence of a certain type of knowledge. He then shows that propositions in the Analytic of Principles are true because they are implied by such knowledge. One writer puts this position as follows:

> The empirically established laws of science presuppose the law of causality, that physical events happen according to universal and necessary causal sequences. Now, if the law of causality did not hold, these physical laws which compose a science of the physical world, would be impossible. Yet, by Kant's fundamental assumption, these laws are accepted as *objektiv gültige*. Hence, the law of causality, as a condition of the possibility of a knowledge of nature, must hold.[19]

This is a typical interpretation of the argument for the second Analogy. Whatever its adequacy in other respects, it fails to show how the second Analogy should be a synthetic proposition or, indeed, why Kant should have thought it to be synthetic. The reconstruction of Kant's argument shows that the second Analogy is true if it is implied by other propositions which are true. But the second Analogy might be implied by the propositions constituting physical science and still be analytic.

19. E. W. Schipper, "Kant's Answer to Hume's Problem," *Kant-Studien*, LIII (1961), 73.

The second way in which Kant's argument has been reconstructed is this. Here we begin, not with the fact of physical science, but with the fact that we pair similar events which tend to be repeated. This fact is then seen to imply Kant's distinction between two kinds of sequence of representations. We entertain a sequence like that of the house which is accidentally ordered. And we also entertain sequences which are irreversible. This distinction implies, according to the present argument, the proposition which Kant identifies as the second Analogy.[20]

Does this argument imply the second Analogy? It does not. I shall assume that the steps in the argument are all valid. But the argument here is fundamentally no different from the preceding one. It does, to be sure, base the deduction, not on the fact of physical science, but rather on a commonplace fact of everyday experience. This change of premises does not explain why the second Analogy should be thought to be synthetic. The propositions which serve as the premises of this argument may imply the truth of the proposition that everything that happens presupposes something upon which it follows by rule. They do not, however, explain why that proposition should be synthetic rather than analytic. So whatever advantage one gains by changing the premises from the propositions of physical science to those of everyday experience, one does not succeed in explaining this crucial feature of the second Analogy.

I am not forgetting that there is an initially plausible defense that somebody holding the position under consideration might offer for that position. My question is why the positions implied by certain common-sense descriptions of the sensuous manifold are synthetic rather than analytic. An answer to this question might be given by saying (1) that all propositions describing common-sense features of the sensuous manifold are synthetic and (2) that all propositions implied by synthetic propositions must themselves be synthetic.

Both of these claims are, I concede, true. But they succeed only in shifting the problem from the synthetic to the alleged *a priori* charac-

20. Lewis White Beck, "Once More Unto the Breach," *Ratio*, IX (1967), 33–37.

ter of the second Analogy. What must be explained now is why the second Analogy is an *a priori* rather than an *a posteriori* proposition; how, that is, the synthetic propositions which are implied by descriptions of common-sense features of the sensuous manifold are any less *a posteriori* than the propositions which imply them. The only way in which this distinction might be drawn on Kantian principles would be by adducing certain facts of pure intuition which are described by synthetic *a priori* propositions. And these facts are, I have been arguing, not available. So the present way of interpreting Kant's argument in the second Analogy does not itself suffice to explain why any propositions implied by contingent (i.e., synthetic *a posteriori*) propositions are both synthetic and *a priori*.

We are left, then, with the implicit theory of judgment to explain how Kant could have thought that what he was endeavoring to prove was a synthetic *a priori* proposition. The second Analogy asserts that there are objects—irreversible time sequences—which fall under the schematized concept of causation. But there is a difficulty with this which, as I hope to show later, pervades Kant's theory of metaphysical propositions. We have not been able to distinguish the sense in which properly causal sequences are irreversible when we regard irreversibility as a characteristic of the pure intuition of time. A similar problem occurred in the case of the first Analogy: The property of pure intuition which was given was not sufficient to show that substances exist. We must therefore examine the specific arguments which Kant gives for both the first and the second Analogies.

✺6✺

Kant's Arguments for the First and Second Analogies

SO FAR I HAVE SHOWN only that the kinds of schemata suggested for the concepts of cause and substance are defective. But this does not exhaust the arguments Kant gives for the first Analogy and the second Analogy. All it does is to show that, whatever else the first Analogy and the second Analogy may or may not show, they do not establish that the concepts of substance and causality have pure intuitions corresponding to them. Now I want to ask what, if anything, Kant's specific arguments for the first Analogy and the second Analogy do establish.

Consider the arguments that Kant offers for the first Analogy. They are basically two. (1) Kant holds that we cannot be aware of change unless what changes is permanent. Kant assumes that we are aware of change even if it is only the successive presentation of the manifold. He argues that, if we were not aware of something permanent, we could not measure the change which takes place when one presentation is succeeded by another in time.[21] (2) The second argument for the first Analogy begins with our knowledge of the simultaneity of events. Kant assumes that we are aware only of a succession of presentations. We can know that what is given to us in the series of presentations which we do know—the various sides of a house, for example—exists at the same time. We could not know this unless continuants existed, from which he concludes that there are substances.[22]

Both of these arguments have the same structure. There are certain propositions asserted about what is called the manifold of presentations. Kant wants to show that propositions of this kind, if true, imply other propositions which assert the existence of substances. But the question to ask here is whether such an implication does obtain. What makes this question hard to answer is the extreme liberality with which Kant uses the word *Vorstellung*. From the examples he gives of a succession of *Vorstellungen*—the sides of a house and the ship moving downstream—it is not clear how much of the object we are given at any time. And this is the root of the difficulty with understanding Kant's arguments for the first Analogy. There is, of course, one way to interpret the propositions which describe the manifold so that they do strictly imply propositions stating that substances exist. In formulating propositions about, say, the sides of a house or the position of a ship, we are asserting something about the presentations

---

21. This is a summary of what Kant says at B224–25.
22. This argument immediately follows the first one at B225–27.

of a certain kind of object. Since objects (as, for example, houses and ships) are given in a series of presentations, propositions describing presentations of boats and houses would imply the existence of something permanent in time.

There are two comments to be made about this argument. The first is that such an argument is circular. It assumes—what Kant has no right to assume at this point—that we are aware of continuants when we are acquainted with presentations. But this is precisely what must be proved. Anyone wanting a proof that continuants exist would not allow the first move in the argument, by which propositions stating what is given in presentations make specific reference to continuants. What Kant is proving is that propositions which describe only the series of presentations constituting what is given in the sensible manifold strictly imply propositions stating the existence of continuants. If my statement of his argument is right, then he assumes in the first move what he has set out to prove. If this first move were not disputed, then why would a proof be necessary?

If we allow Kant the assumption made in the first move of the argument, then the implication which is wanted does obtain. This introduces the second comment. The proposition that continuants exist can be only a synthetic *a posteriori* proposition. To think that it is synthetic *a priori* is to conflate an *a priori* but analytic proposition with a proposition that is synthetic but *a posteriori*. The only *a priori* proposition is the one formulating the inference from propositions stating something about the manifold of sensibility to propositions stating the existence of continuants. The proposition stating this inference is *a priori* because it is analytic: Its denial generates a contradiction. The conclusion of the inference is, however, synthetic: The claim that there are continuants can be denied without contradiction. Is such a claim *a priori*? I think not. For we cannot know whether such a claim is true or false independently of experience. Nor, for that matter, can we know that it is universally and necessarily true. Both of these conclusions follow from my argument that the schema of substance cannot be either a pure intuition or a property of pure intuition. To assert that the existence of substance follows from facts about the sensible manifold is to assert a proposition whose truth or falsity can be ascertained *a priori* only if the characteristics of the manifold from which this proposition was inferred were characteristics of pure intuition.

The argument for the second Analogy parallels Kant's argument for the first Analogy. He begins by introducing certain propositions about the manifold and then goes on to ask what they imply. All apprehension of the manifold is successive. But there is a distinction which separates certain kinds of succession from others. Some sequences are marked by the irreversibility of their time relations. And this implies that there are causal relations in the manifold.[23]

My interest in this argument is a restricted one. I propose to grant that the establishment of irreversible sequences is sufficient to establish the existence of causal relations. The only question I wish to raise about the argument is how it proves a proposition that is synthetic and *a priori*. The argument does not yield such a proposition as its conclusion. To show that there are causal sequences is to establish that the existence of irreversible time relations implies the existence of causal sequences. The existence of irreversible time relations would be a necessary and universal condition of our experience of objects only if it were a characteristic of the relations between pure intuitions. Now if irreversibility is, as I have already argued, a characteristic of pure intuition, then it is a characteristic which belongs to causal and non-causal sequences alike. If it is separated from pure intuition, then irreversibility will not be a universal and necessary condition of our experience of objects. What is proved by the argument for the second Analogy, then, is something very different from a synthetic *a priori*

---

23. What I have summarized here as one proof is presented in Norman Kemp Smith, *A Commentary to Kant's* Critique of Pure Reason (New York: Humanities Press, 1962), pp. 371–81, as a series of five. Whatever else may distinguish parts of Kant's discussion, all of those parts depend upon the distinction between kinds of succession. This is why I speak of only one argument here. For if Kant is unable to exhibit the distinction between two kinds of succession in intuition, he will not be able to show that there is anything in experience which falls under the concept of causality; hence, he will not be able to show that the second Analogy, understood as a synthetic *a priori* proposition, is true.

proposition. There is, first, a synthetic *a posteriori* proposition which states the existence of causal sequences. And there is, secondly, the analytic proposition which states the relation of implication between sequences that are irreversible and those that are causal.

The examination of Kant's specific arguments for the first and second Analogies shows how dependent they are upon showing that what is being established is a characteristic of pure intuition or relations between pure intuitions. What the arguments must show, if they are to establish conclusions that hold for our experience of any object in our manifold, is that there are certain characteristics which are present in any experience. This can be shown only by establishing that every claim about the manifold entails the truth of other claims which state such characteristics. As it is, however, what is shown by both the argument for the first Analogy and that for the second is that certain features of our manifold entail the existence of other kinds of features. Even if this entailment holds, the resulting conclusion, although synthetic, is not *a priori*. For such arguments do not establish that these characteristics are strictly universal features of our experience.

⟨7⟩

An Alternative Interpretation of Kant's Argument

UP TO NOW I have been arguing against the view that the first and second Analogies are shown by Kant to be synthetic *a priori* propositions. I have, however, made certain assumptions about the character of the argument Kant must present if he is to prove this. I have, for example, assumed that any such proof must exhibit in pure intuition objects which fall under the concepts of substance and causality. And I have examined the arguments he gives as though he were in fact trying to supply such objects. The structural motive for this procedure is clear. If Kant wants to show that either Analogy is synthetic, he must show that the concept involved in each has corresponding pure intuitions falling under it. Similarly, if Kant wants to show that we can know *a priori* that both analogies are true, the objects which fall under the pure concepts involved must be temporal or spatial properties. Yet, on the assumptions I have made, Kant is unable to show that either Analogy expresses a synthetic *a priori* proposition.

There is, however, another interpretation that can be given to the arguments for the first and second Analogies. I propose to show what this interpretation is and that it has considerable textual support. I shall only then ask whether this way of interpreting the arguments can show that either Analogy expresses a proposition that is synthetic *a priori*.

I begin by outlining the alternative interpretation of the second Analogy. Kant wants to show that we must conceive of events as ordered or we will not have conceived of them as causally related. This connection must, it is held, be temporal. But the causal connection need not be perceived by us. In fact, on the present interpretation, it cannot be. For all we are given is a series. And it is our task to order that series. We succeed in ordering it when we have connected it according to a rule.

If this interpretation of Kant's procedure in the argument for the second Analogy be accepted, we will have to abandon the assumptions previously made about the character of his argument. For, on this alternative interpretation, Kant does not have to show us that we are given an objective sequence as a property of temporal sequences. All he has to do is to show us how we arrive at an experience of objective sequence by applying the category to temporal sequences. On the previous interpretation of the argument, it was assumed that Kant must make the distinction between the two kinds of sequence in terms of the properties of time. On the present interpretation, however, the distinction between an arbitrary and an irreversible temporal order is made in terms of the application of a rule to a temporal sequence. The distinction is not, in other words, made by locating a property of time by which the two kinds of sequence can be distinguished but rather by showing that a rule governs our synthesis of a causal sequence, whereas no such rule is present in the synthesis of a noncausal sequence.

This, then, is the interpretation. What textual support does it have? One passage supporting it occurs at B234. When I am presented with a series of appearances, Kant says, "I am conscious only that my imagination sets the one state before and the other after, not that the one state precedes the other in the object. In other words, the objective relation of appearances that follow upon one another is not determined through mere perception." What Kant holds here is that we cannot, by tracing out relations between temporal sequences, determine which sequence is causal. Yet, if causal relations in our experience are not given to us by certain kinds of temporal sequence, how do we distinguish between a causal and a merely temporal sequence? The answer to this question is given at B236, where Kant says that what distinguishes the one from the other is a rule by which the one can be combined. Noncausal sequences do not stand under a rule. They can be combined in any way you please.

Both of these passages suggest the following interpretation. It is wrong to look for a property of time to distinguish between the two kinds of sequences. For what distinguishes them is a rule, not a property of time. Thus, all that Kant must do in his argument for the second Analogy is to show that we invoke rules when we make the distinction between causal and noncausal sequences. He is not constrained to supply a property of pure intuition to perform this task.

This interpretation of Kant's argument in the Analogies derives addtional support from two other sources. The first is the general characterization that Kant gives of transcendental propositions:

> Synthetic propositions in regard to *things* in general, the intuition of which does not admit of being given *a priori*, are transcendental. . . . But these synthetic principles cannot exhibit *a priori* any one of their concepts in a specific instance; they can only do this *a posteriori*, by means of experience, which itself is possible only in conformity with these principles.[24]

If the second Analogy is a transcendental proposition in this sense, then it follows that there will be no *a priori* intuition that exhibits the

24. A720–21 = B748–49.

concept of causality. Irreversibility of time relations will not, accordingly, be an *a priori* intuition which instantiates causality. The only instantiations will be empirical.

But how is the second Analogy proved, if there is no *a priori* intuition corresponding to it? The answer to this question is contained in the notion of the possibility of experience. And this is the second source from which the alternative interpretation derives support. A concept can, on this view, be shown to apply to experience as a condition of our experience of objects. We have shown that causality applies to experience when we have shown that it gives a rule for the synthesis of empirical objects. And this is different from showing that the rule associated with the concept prescribes a procedure of synthesis for pure intuition.[25]

Apply this interpretation, finally, to the examples which Kant gives of temporal sequence. The first sequence is arbitrary, determined by the changing position of the observer. The second is not arbitrary because no movement of the observer can alter the order in which the events present themselves to him. The difference between these two sequences would not, on the interpretation under consideration, lie in any property of time itself. The difference lies only in the way we think about the movement of the ship, which is causal because we order the sequence so that it cannot be reversed without surrendering its claim to be causal. All that intuition gives us is a sequence in imagination. What transforms some of those sequences which we combine in imagination into causal sequences is that we think of them as causal.

I omit consideration of the present interpretation in the context of the first Analogy. It would be strictly parallel to the interpretation given of the second Analogy: The concept of substance would not have a pure intuition corresponding to it but would be applicable to sequences of representations which we conceive as parts of a permanent substratum through time. The strategy of each of the arguments would, then, be the same. Kant would be showing that we have a

25. Cf. A156 = B196.

right to employ a category by showing that it enables us to conceive of certain sequences in our manifold in certain ways.

The alternative interpretation has two major defects. Its textual support is unsatisfactory and, if it is attributed to Kant, such an interpretation would contradict other things he says. Consider the textual foundation for the present interpretation. The first passage which appears to support it is Kant's statement in the proof of the second Analogy that the objective relation of appearances is not determined through mere perception. Does this passage say that there is nothing in the manifold of pure intuition to correspond to causal sequences? I think not. The sense in which an objective time order is not perceivable is that an examination of *empirical* intuitions will not yield any perception of the proper ordering relation. There is nothing about the perceptions of a ship at various times during its trip down-stream that enables me to decide which presentation should be ordered prior to another. It does not follow, however, that there is nothing at all in pure intuition which orders the relation in which those empirical intuitions are ordered. This is why the passage cannot be used to support the conclusion that the category of cause has no pure intuition corresponding to it.

But there is a second passage, in which Kant appears to deny that a transcendental proposition has any pure intuition corresponding to it. This appears to support the view that the second Analogy has no pure intuitions to which it refers but is proved only because it states a condition for the possibility of experience. But the passage in question and others like it make this claim only for propositions that concern objects in general. But neither the first nor the second Analogy is about objects in general. Both of them contain schematized categories. And these concern only our manifold. So if the passage is to be of any use in supporting the claim that no intuition corresponds to the categories of substance and cause as they appear in the Analytic, a new proof must be given; a proof, namely, that propositions containing schematized categories refer to objects in general. Such a proof obviously cannot be given; for what, on Kant's view, distinguished a schematized from a pure category is that the former, unlike the latter, refers only to possible objects of our manifold and therefore cannot refer to objects in general.[26]

This is not all. An acceptance of the interpretation under consideration will involve its advocates in two serious problems about reconciling their interpretation with other things Kant says. The first such difficulty results from the claim, basic to the present interpretation, that the categories enable us to conceive of objects as distinct from sequences of representations. Thus we are obliged to think of an objective sequence in time as a succession which accords with a rule; and we must think of the representations in the manifold as presentations of something that is permanent in time if we are to conceive of an object of experience. This is, however, evidence that both the first and second Analogies are analytic. For both of them state the conditions under which we are said correctly to conceive of an object of experience. And the conditions of correct conception of anything are parts of the concept which we apply to the object we conceive. This makes both Analogies analytic. It has the further disadvantage of making it unintelligible why Kant should have offered proofs for them. If he sets out merely to show what is contained within a concept, then what he will have shown if he succeeds is only something about our thought of objects. He will not have shown that there must be something in experience corresponding to them.

This presents us with the second problem. Even if Kant succeeds in showing that substance and causality are conditions of the possibility of our experience of objects, he will not have succeeded in proving

---

26. There are passages in which Kant implicitly distinguishes between transcendental propositions referring to objects in general and those which refer to particular kinds of objects, when he says (A135 = B174) that "transcendental philosophy has the peculiarity that besides the rule . . . , which is given in the pure concept of the understanding, it can also specify *a priori* the instance to which the rule is applied. . . . It must formulate by means of universal but sufficient marks the conditions under which objects can be given in harmony with those concepts." What he is saying here is that pure concepts are to be distinguished from those concepts which refer to the kinds of objects which can, depending on the character of our sensibility, be given to us for subsumption under pure concepts.

that they are any more than conditions of our thought about objects as distinct from conditions which belong universally and necessarily to our experience of the objects in our manifold. Thus it is possible for Kant to show that every object in our experience must conform to certain rules if it is to be counted as an object without showing that there are any objects which fall under the concepts he is analyzing. And so it would be possible, on the present interpretation, for Kant to show that every object must be conceived in a certain way and still not show that there is anything in our manifold which falls under the concept of object. Yet this is Kant's intention in the Analytic of Principles. What he attempts to prove is that the propositions which constitute the Principles state conditions of experience which are necessary and universal conditions of objects.[27] Kant cannot establish this until he has established that the objects which we experience conform to the Principles of the Analytic. And he cannot demonstrate this by showing what we count as the conditions of conceiving objects. Any such account that might be offered must be supplemented by a proof that there are objects which fall under the subject concepts of such propositions. This is the second difficulty which results from attributing the view under consideration to Kant: Kant will have shown that we are constrained to think of the conditions of there being an object of experience; but he will not have shown that there is anything in our experience which corresponds to these conditions. Since Kant purports to show that all objects of our experience must conform to these accounts, any interpretation of his position which omits that fact must falsify what Kant undertakes to do in the Analytic.

8

Conclusion

WE ARE THUS LEFT with the following account of the Analogies. They are synthetic propositions only if they are interpreted according to the hidden or implicit criterion of syntheticity. And what makes

27. A158 = B197.

them metaphysical propositions is not that they contain concepts which are about an object in general but that they contain concepts which refer only to phenomenal objects. The objects which, on the implicit criterion, fall under these concepts are relations which obtain among pure intuitions.

The evidence that what I have just summarized is in fact Kant's argument is complicated. Part of this evidence derives, as I have argued, from the presence of a new criterion of judgment in the *Kritik* which stands side by side with the one Kant explicitly adopts. Another part of the evidence comes from the shift which takes place in the argument of the chapter on schematism—the shift from a discussion of pure to schematized concepts. But this evidence alone is based on a departure in several crucial respects from the description Kant himself gives of what he is doing. This is why I further relied upon an argument which showed that, if we take that description at face value, we cannot explain why Kant should have thought that synthetic propositions are not reducible to analytic propositions, or why transcendental propositions must be synthetic *a priori* rather than analytic, or why Kant should have thought that intuition was at all relevant in establishing the applicability of synthetic *a priori* propositions in metaphysics to our manifold.

Kant's solution to the verification of synthetic propositions in metaphysics is, then, different from what it has usually been taken to be. He seeks to verify such propositions by showing that they state the necessary conditions for the possibility of experiencing objects. And this is shown by supplying characteristics of pure intuition which correspond to the concepts which constitute the thought of an object in general. If these concepts can be instantiated by pure intuition, then it follows that they universally and necessarily apply to objects of our experience. This is possible because pure intuition is a formal condition of our being presented with any phenomenal objects. And to show that such a condition has certain properties is automatically to show that any objects which are presented to us under that condition will share these characteristics. That is Kant's solution of the problem of how metaphysical propositions are verifiable.

But there is something wrong with this solution as it applies to the examples which Kant gives. Kant tells us that duration, succession, and coexistence are the three modes of time.[28] These are the characteristics of pure intuition which, if Kant's solution is correct, must be made to correspond to the three concepts of substance, cause, and reciprocity.[29] But these characteristics are not adequate to the concepts which they are meant to instantiate. Duration is present in our experience of objects because of time. But the sense in which time endures is not the sense in which substances endure. Time is permanent with respect to the changes that go on within it. Substances are permanent *through* time. Hence time cannot be the exhibition of what we think in the concept of substance.

The same point can be made for the concept of cause. The property of time called succession cannot be adequate to the concept of cause because succession is a characteristic of all manifolds, both causal and noncausal. And so the concept of cause cannot be shown in this way to be a universal and necessary condition of our experience of objects. The concepts which are identified as properly metaphysical must therefore be changed or they cannot be shown to contain universal and necessary features of our experience of objects.

The result of this is to bring into clear focus the difficulty that attends Kant's theory of synthetic *a priori* propositions in metaphysics. This theory has been attacked in two ways that have since become standard. Critics of the theory have either argued that Kant was mistaken in thinking that there are propositions in metaphysics that are synthetic *a priori* or that, even if there be such propositions, there is no way to show that they are adequate to our concept of what an experiential object is. It can be shown, I think, that both of these lines of objection are based on mistakes and, further, that they do not touch the jugular vein of Kant's theory.

The first line of objection runs like this. What is wrong with Kant's theory of the synthetic *a priori*, it is argued, is that the very proposi-

28. B219.
29. I omit discussion of the concept of reciprocity here for reasons which I have given at the beginning of this chapter.

tions which are asserted by Kant to be synthetic are not the same propositions which Kant seeks to verify *a priori*.[30] The strategy of this line of objection can be best seen by reference to the examples of substance and cause. As both the concepts of substance and cause occur in propositions which Kant takes to be synthetic, they respectively connote "that which is subject and cannot be predicate" and "that in the absence of which a thing could not be." Thus neither of these concepts entails any temporal determination, since they apply indifferently to temporal and nontemporal objects. The predicates of the synthetic propositions in which they occur do connote temporal determinations. But the propositions which Kant actually attempts to demonstrate in the Analytic of Principles contain narrower concepts of substance and cause. Thus the concept of substance as it figures in the Analytic does entail a temporal determination; and so does the concept of cause. Hence, this objection concludes, Kant can give *a priori* proofs of propositions in metaphysics only because such propositions are tacitly analytic.

If the exegetical position which I argued earlier is at all sound, this line of objection does not touch the Kantian theory of synthetic *a priori* propositions in metaphysics. Such propositions do, admittedly, contain concepts which are narrower than the ones which Kant identifies elsewhere in the *Kritik* as metaphysical. But it does not follow that the propositions are analytic, for they claim that objects fall under those concepts, not that one concept lies outside the scope of another. And the argument that such propositions are analytic depends entirely on the viability of Kant's claim that expressions for intuitions cannot be constructed out of expressions for concepts. And so this kind of attack on Kant's theory cannot be sustained. For it does not show that there are no synthetic *a priori* propositions in metaphysics. It shows only that there are no such propositions if Kant's theory is grounded on the conception of a synthetic proposition which is given by the manifest theory of judgment. The effect of this kind of

30. The classical statement of this kind of objection is in C. I. Lewis' *An Analysis of Knowledge and Valuation* (La Salle, Ill.: Open Court, 1962), pp. 157 ff.

objection, then, is to reflect our attention from the adequacy of the theory which is present in Kant's text to the one which we are led to believe is there on a particular interpretation of it.

There is a second line of attack on Kant's theory of synthetic *a priori* propositions in metaphysics which differs from the one I have just sketched in that it leaves open the possibility of synthetic *a priori* propositions but argues that what Kant must show is that the set of such propositions he proposes is adequate to the concept of what we must count as an object of our experience.[31] The complaint here is that, even though Kant can prove certain synthetic *a priori* propositions in metaphysics, he cannot show that they are the only propositions which must be true if we are to experience perceptual objects. And in the absence of such a proof, it is argued, other sets of propositions might equally well serve as analyses of an object in general. But unless Kant can supply this missing proof, he will not have shown that the propositions which he proves are conditions of an object in general. And it is only if he can do this that he can show that they are properly metaphysical propositions.

This objection derives whatever plausibility it has from the defects of Kant's Metaphysical Deduction. There he does attempt to list all of the concepts which collectively constitute the content of our over-reaching concept of an object in general. What is interesting about this attempt is that Kant's case for the synthetic *a priori* in metaphysics does not rest on the success of the Metaphysical Deduction. That the theory which he propounds in the Analytic of Principles does not, finally, rest upon the Metaphysical Deduction is due entirely to the shift of Kant's argument in the chapter of schematism. Thus Kant's claim that the synthetic *a priori* propositions he seeks to prove in the Analytic are adequate to what we would count as a perceptual object does not rest on a proof that such propositions state the only condi-

31. A brief statement of this objection is to be found in Ledger Wood's essay, "The Transcendental Method," in G. T. Whitney and David F. Bowers (eds.), *The Heritage of Kant* (Princeton: Princeton University Press, 1939), pp. 33–34. The most sustained form of the objection is found in C. I. Lewis' classic, *Mind and the World Order* (New York: Scribner's, 1929).

tions of perceptual objects. And that Kant did not, moreover, attempt such a proof is the result of his distinction between the phenomenal and noumenal worlds. Part of what he means by making this distinction is that it is possible for us to experience other manifolds of sensibility. But if this is possible, then he cannot be saying that the synthetic *a priori* propositions he seeks to prove in metaphysics are exhaustive statements of what is to count as an object in general. Thus this line of attack on Kant's theory fails, for Kant simply concedes the point at issue. The strength of the theory he offers rests upon his ability to show that the propositions he offers state universal and necessary characteristics of objects, not upon his ability—the possession of which he specifically disavows—to show that these propositions are true for every kind of object which can be presented in any kind of manifold.

Both of the standard attacks on the doctrine of the Analogies miss the mark. One overlooks the fact, crucial to that doctrine, that propositions are synthetic because of the relation they have to intuition. The other overlooks the fact, equally crucial to that doctrine, that the success of Kant's proof depends upon his ability to show that the concepts involved in metaphysical propositions contain elements which refer to necessary and universal characteristics of intuition. But the Analogies do depend upon Kant's ability to relate metaphysical concepts to intuitions which instantiate them. And the problem with this account of verification in metaphysics is that the pure intuitions which must instantiate metaphysical concepts are too impoverished to instantiate them exactly. So there may, indeed, be synthetic *a priori* propositions associated with metaphysics; but that they depend upon a doctrine of pure intuition which cannot sustain them is the problem which Kant's account does not solve.

CHAPTER SIX

Ontology and the

Transcendental

Method

MY DISCUSSION OF KANT'S REFORM of metaphysical method has thus far been restricted to two paradigm cases of metaphysical propositions. Both of these propositions have been associated with a distinctive method by which, according to Kant, they can be proved. I have not tried to show what this method is, preferring to restrict myself to the specific arguments Kant offers for the first and second Analogies. What I propose to undertake now is a general examination of the transcendental method in the first *Kritik* as it relates to propositions in metaphysics. There are, as I have tried to show, problems associated with the proofs Kant offers for certain examples of metaphysical propositions. Perhaps these problems are peculiar to the propositions Kant tries to prove and are not endemic to the transcendental method itself.

But Kant himself does not give us a general statement of what that method is. I shall leave open the question whether Kant practices the same method in all three critiques and ask only what that method is when it is applied to the verification of propositions about an object in general. The account I offer of that method will be divided into four stages. First I shall state the characteristics which, on Kant's theory, any metaphysical proposition must have. This will provide the basis for explaining the method appropriate to the proof of such propositions. The second stage will consist in the classification of ways in which the transcendental method either has been expounded in the literature on Kant or to which Kant's own statements might invite interpretation. The third stage will be an account of that method which will be free from the defects of previous views. And finally I shall try to show the strengths and limitations of that method as a way of deciding metaphysical propositions.

❧ I ❧
The Marks of a Metaphysical Proposition

THE PROBLEM KANT RAISED with metaphysical propositions derives entirely from two peculiarities which they allegedly have. All such propositions are universal and necessary as well as being claims about what exists. It is essential to see why Kant requires any such proposition to have both of these characteristics. The reason Kant requires them to be universal and necessary is familiar: What they assert concerns all objects and not merely a subset of such objects. If metaphysical propositions lacked this characteristic, then no metaphysical proposition could be distinguished from high-level empirical generalizations. A generalization of this sort would not tell us the essential marks of an object of experience as such. And even if we do generalize about just these characteristics of an object, the defect of any such claim about the characteristics of an object as such is that it tells us something only about observed characteristics of objects. And so, even if the proposition did concern strictly general characteristics of an object, it could not be a claim that these characteristics are strictly general; hence, it could not be a metaphysical claim.

There is another feature of metaphysical propositions which is formulated in the demand that they be strictly universal but which is obscured when Kant calls both propositions in metaphysics and those in mathematics synthetic *a priori*. There are two kinds of strict universality. A proposition can be strictly universal if it states a characteristic of all objects of a certain class. But it does not follow that all objects will have such a characteristic. Thus there are two ways in which a synthetic claim which is *a priori* does not have an exception. The claim can state a truth that governs a limited class of objects. Or it can state a truth that governs every object just insofar as it is an object. The former is obviously a more restricted kind of universality, while only the latter is present in metaphysics. Now there is a good reason why this distinction is obscured in Kant: All of the propositions which he cites as paradigm cases of synthetic *a priori* propositions are either mathematical or metaphysical. And both of these propositions refer to intuition, the characteristics of which are bound to belong to every object because the characteristics of pure intuition will belong to every phenomenal object. But the distinction remains: What distinguishes the universality of metaphysical propositions from that of propositions in mathematics is that the former refer to all objects while the latter do not.

But necessity and universality are not sufficient to qualify a proposition as metaphysical. Such a proposition must also be about existence. This is a characteristic which Kant does not emphasize in his discussion of the synthetic *a priori*.[1] But that such a characteristic must attach to propositions is implied by what he says concerning analytic propositions. The relevant part of the theory of analyticity is that no analytic proposition can be about what exists. This follows from the fact that the truth of all analytic propositions is independent of what there is. Thus to show that a proposition is analytic as Kant under-

---

1. He does, however, say this by implication when he makes such statements as "Metaphysics . . . considers whatever is in so far as *it is*" (A845 = B873).

stands the notion is to show only that the predicate concept applies to the same objects as the subject concept. And such a proposition can be true even if there are no objects at all or if the objects that there are have a very different character from the relation asserted in the analytic proposition. This truth should not be obscured either by the charge that such an interpretation of analytic propositions would make them into propositions about words or concepts as distinct from objects or by the charge that Kant himself gives a schematic representation of an analytic proposition in which he specifically says that both subject and predicate concepts are about an object.[2]

To say that an analytic proposition is not a truth about objects does not imply that it must be a truth about concepts or words. All analytic propositions are about the objects which belong to the extension of their subject concepts. But this is different from being about existent objects. However you analyze the notion of an existent object, you must distinguish between an object as part of the extension of a concept and an object as existent. This is just the commonplace that existence claims cannot be deduced from claims expressing relations between concepts.

Nor does the fact that Kant's schematic representation of analytic propositions involves a reference to an object show that Kant thought analytic propositions to be about objects. All that this shows is that even an analytic judgment involves a reference of concepts to objects. But this is compatible with saying that the objects to which concepts are referred in analytic judgments are objects only in that they belong to the extension of the class marked out by the subject concepts of such propositions. And this no more shows that analytic propositions are about existent objects or objects of possible experience than to say that I have a concept of the fourth angle of a Euclidean triangle shows that such a concept is about an existent object.

2. Cf. *Nachlass*, No. 3128: "Each judgment means to assert: everything, to which the concept of the subject belongs, to it the predicate also belongs. This can occur when the predicate is identical with the concept of the subject, as in analytic propositions, or also when not, as in synthetic propositions. The subject is something, x. The concept of it is S, the predicate P." Cf. also *Nachlass*, Nos. 3921, 3964, and 4052.

There is only one more suspicion that must be removed in order to show that analytic propositions cannot, on Kant's theory, be about objects. Consider the admittedly analytic proposition, "All bachelors are unmarried males." Since this is analytic, it will not be about objects. But let us, further, suppose that we have discovered that there are bachelors as objects of experience which fall under the concept "bachelor." Does this not show that analytic propositions are about objects? For does this not prove that the analytic proposition under consideration is about existent objects? It does not. What it proves is that the proposition is about existent and nonexistent objects indifferently. It does not follow that it is about objects insofar as they are existent.

What it means to say that analytic propositions are not about objects comes, then, to this. You are denying that such propositions are about existent as distinct from nonexistent or possible objects. You are not, it should be added, denying that analytic propositions are about objects at all. And it would be a mistake to think that the present position about analytic propositions commits Kant to the position that analytic propositions are about nothing at all. It would, however, be an equally great mistake to conclude from the position that analytic propositions are about possible objects that they tell us something about the world. This inference is fallacious just because the truth of an analytic proposition is compatible with there being nothing at all in the world of the kind of object to which the subject concept refers. And this is what is being denied when it is said that analytic propositions are not propositions about existence.

But one of the marks of a metaphysical proposition is that it makes a claim about existence. This does not mean that there are no analytic propositions in metaphysics. But this does not make such propositions distinctively metaphysical. Hence the marks of metaphysical propositions are that they are claims which are strictly universal and that they are claims about what exists. These are the requirements which, on Kant's theory, metaphysical propositions must fulfill. They are also requirements which any proposition proved by the transcendental method in the first *Kritik* must fulfill.

⟨ϵ⟩ 2 ⟨϶⟩

Accounts of the Transcendental Method

I DISTINGUISH FOUR DIFFERENT ACCOUNTS of the transcendental method in the first *Kritik*. These are either views which can be found in the literature on Kant or which some of the remarks Kant makes about that method suggest.

1. This first account of the transcendental method deals with what counts as a necessary condition of experience.[3] Kant begins with ordinary experience, in which we take substances and causes to exist, and separates what we find in this experience into sense *qualia*, the spatial and temporal arrangement of these *qualia*, and the categorial relations in which *qualia* stand.[4] This separation is governed by what Kant takes to be those elements in common-sense experience which are necessary in that their absence would make experience impossible. Thus the general procedure of proof of a metaphysical proposition would, on this account, come to this. We begin by distinguishing sense *qualia* from the formal features of experience. And we show that the propositions which formulate the applicability of these formal elements are true because they are implied by propositions which describe sense *qualia*. The resultant propositions are synthetic and *a priori*.

Let us begin the assessment of this account by asking what a sense *quale* would be in Kant's terminology. The closest corresponding term is "sensation," by which Kant understands "a perception which related itself solely to the subject as the modification of its state."[5] But this does not square with the examples of what would apparently be sensations in the Analytic of Principles. For there he gives the exam-

---

3. Ledger Wood, "The Transcendental Method," in G. T. Whitney and David F. Bowers (eds.), *The Heritage of Kant* (Princeton: Princeton University Press, 1939), *passim*, gives the best statement of this view of the transcendental method known to me.

4. *Ibid.*, p. 33.

5. A320 = B376; cf. *Inaugural Dissertation*, para. 4 (*Werke*, II).

ples of the successive positions of a ship and the successive presentations of the sides of a house.[6] A description of the representations
which are presented to me would not be a description of sensations but
of presentations which any observer can entertain. This is so even in
the case of the successive representation of the sides of a house: what
is subjective is the choice of the *order* in which I choose to view the
house, not the part of the house that I may be viewing. Thus what
would count in Kant's terminology as a sense *quale* would not be a
representation of something subjective but rather of a part of an
object.

Descriptions of these presentations would, then, be descriptions of
sense *qualia*. But do such descriptions imply propositions asserting the
existence of categorical features of experience? It seems clear that
they do not. The mere description of *qualia* or representations which
are presented successively to the mind does not imply the existence of
permanent entities through time or causal interaction. That any such
group of representations is presented to me is compatible with there
being no permanent element in experience as well as there being no
causal connection. Thus if the transcendental method is conceived as it
is on this first account, it would be useless in establishing any proposition about categorial features at all, much less propositions about
those features that are synthetic and *a priori*.

And Kant did not hold this view of the transcendental method. He
says that "the appearances, insofar as they are objects of consciousness
simply in virtue of being representations, are not in any way distinct
from their apprehension." [7] And if this is so, description of the series
of our representations simply as objects of consciousness will not yield
conclusions about categorial features. Otherwise an inspection of these
representations would yield categorial features and we would be able
to distinguish between representations as they are objects of consciousness and as they are objective appearances by simple inspection of the
manifold.

6. A190 = B235 ff.
7. A190 = B235; cf. A90 = B122: "For appearances can certainly be
given in intuition independently of functions of the intellect."

2. The second account of the transcendental method is in part an attempt to repair the difficulties of the preceding account.[8] Here sense *qualia* are replaced by our ordinary experience of the world or the empirical knowledge we have about this experience. Thus a transcendental argument starts with a set of propositions constituting a body of scientific knowledge; and the conclusion of such an argument is a set of propositions which are necessary conditions of the truth of propositions contained in the first set.[9]

The advantage of characterizing the transcendental method in this way is twofold. For one thing, it escapes the obvious difficulty of saying that the propositions implying transcendental propositions are descriptions of sense *qualia*. Here we begin either with descriptions of the world of common-sense perception or with propositions formulating laws governing the objects of common sense. Both start, that is, from full-fledged objects of experience. For another, Kant himself lends support to this view. He says that transcendental propositions are verified by showing that they are conditions of the possibility of experience.[10] And when he talks about the possibility of experience, Kant indicates that he means the possibility of empirical knowledge, as when he says that "empirical knowledge is experience." [11]

But there is none the less a grave defect in this account of the transcendental method. It wrongly assumes that in establishing the necessary conditions of the truth of propositions constituting certain bodies of knowledge, Kant believes that he is establishing the necessary conditions for experience of an object in general. It is true that Kant concludes from the truth of the transcendental propositions he seeks to prove that an explanation can be given of how certain propositions in the natural sciences and mathematics are true. But the proofs

---

8. A good but little-known statement of this view is found in Max Scheler, *Die Transzendentale und die psychologische Methode* (Leipzig: Dürr, 1900), pp. 37 ff.

9. Cf. *ibid.*, p. 37: "Den Ausgangspunkt bilden wissenschaftliche Urteile, resp. Systeme solcher, und nicht um deren Ursachen wird gefragt, sondern um deren logische Gründe."

10. A156 = B195.

11. B165; cf. B218.

that he offers in the Analytic of Principles do not contain the assumption that the propositions of the natural sciences are true. All of Kant's proofs there begin from our experience of a perceptual object. Only after he has established the synthetic *a priori* proposition in the Analytic on other grounds does Kant introduce propositions of natural science and mathematics, the truth of which is an alleged consequence of the truth of the transcendental propositions he seeks to prove.

Let us, then, assume that Kant begins, not with propositions about the sciences, but with propositions about ordinary perceptual objects. Will this change in the present account of the transcendental method show how Kant can generate synthetic *a priori* propositions as conclusions? The answer is that it will not. Changing the basic propositions of the method from those of the sciences to those of common sense merely creates another difficulty to beset this account of the method. If Kant is seeking to show that propositions describing our experience of *objects* imply transcendental propositions, then the method will be flatly circular. This can be shown as follows. At the beginning of his proof for the second Analogy, Kant distinguishes two senses of "object." First, anything is an object if it is merely present to our consciousness. Secondly, however, an "object" stands for the commonsensical objects of our perceptual world.[12] And part of what distinguishes the latter kind of object is that the concept we have of such an object includes the categories. To claim acquaintance with a commonsensical perceptual object is in part to claim acquaintance with something that endures through time and has causal antecedents. Thus if Kant were to establish the truth of propositions asserting the applicability of the categories to objects by deducing such propositions from propositions claiming the existence of commonsensical objects, he would be assuming the applicability of the very categories about which this must be proved.

Nor did Kant hold this view. He does say that the truth of transcendental propositions is shown when it can be shown that they

12. B234 ff.

make empirical knowledge possible. But this does not force the conclusion that he deductively infers from the truth of propositions
claiming the existence of empirical objects to the truth of transcendental propositions. You can show that a transcendental proposition is
true because what it claims is a necessary condition of propositions
which are themselves not claims about the existence of objects but
which entail such claims. A transcendental proof would, accordingly,
proceed from claims about objects as contents of awareness, move to
transcendental propositions as necessary conditions of these claims,
and only then move to claims about common-sense objects—the truth
of which claims would be a deductive consequence of the truth of the
transcendental propositions. And this is the procedure Kant actually
follows in the proofs for the Analogies. He begins with a certain set
of propositions about objects understood merely as contents of awareness. He then tries to show that these propositions imply other
propositions which are about objects. And it is only with regard to
these latter propositions that transcendental propositions are shown to
apply. This is admittedly a sketchy view of Kant's procedure. All I
wish to show, however, is that the present view of that procedure
falsifies it in a crucial respect: We are wrongly asked to believe that
the transcendental method begins with propositions about common-
sense perceptual objects.

  3. The foregoing accounts seem to exhaust the possibilities. We
take the transcendental method to begin with propositions about
either sense *qualia* or common-sense perceptual objects. If we take the
former alternative, no relation of implication obtains between those
propositions and what Kant identifies as a transcendental proposition.
And if we take the latter alternative, we have a relation of deductive
implication between the propositions with which the method begins
and those with which it ends. But the deductive relation we get is the
result of making the method plainly circular. There is, however, a
third account of the method that does not involve the assumption that
the relation between the propositions with which the method begins
and those with which it ends is one of deduction. Here the notion of
necessary condition is explicated in terms of presupposition. What is

denied on the present account is that the truth of certain empirical propositions implies the truth of transcendental propositions.[13] Empirical propositions presuppose transcendental propositions but do not imply them. Let p stand for any empirical proposition and q stand for any transcendental proposition; p is said to presuppose q if and only if q is a necessary condition of the truth or falsity of p. Any value of q will thus be deducible from the truth or falsity of p.[14]

What distinguishes the third account of the method is that even the denial of empirical propositions implies the truth of transcendental propositions. But this account only slightly obscures the problems present in the foregoing accounts. The sense in which either the truth or falsity of empirical propositions assumes the truth of transcendental propositions is this: To deny an empirical proposition is to deny that this or that continuant exists or that this or that causal nexus exists. But this is not to deny the existence of *all* continuants or *all* causal connections. Thus the falsity of the denial would, on this account, still imply the existence of causal connections or continuants. The only way in which this implication could obtain is if the existence of either causal connections or continuants were made the assumption of either such a denial or such an affirmation. But this is precisely what the method seeks to prove. So this account has the defect of the second account: It does not explain how the assumption which is part of both affirmation and denial of the existence of particular elements in experience is justified in the first place. And this is what makes the account circular.

4. There is another account of the transcendental method according to which a transcendental proposition is verified when we can show that it is presupposed by its own denial. The account I am about to consider is based on the notion of presupposition but none the less differs from the third account. On the present account the denial of a transcendental proposition is said to presuppose the truth of that

13. A representative statement of this view is found in Patricia A. Crawford, "Kant's Theory of Philosophical Proof," *Kant-Studien*, LIII (1961–62), 257–68.
14. *Ibid.*, p. 266.

proposition. On the third account, it will be remembered, the denial or assertion of an empirical proposition was held to presuppose the truth of the transcendental proposition. The present view of transcendental arguments has been forcefully argued by P. F. Strawson in *Individuals*. He does not, however, claim that the view of transcendental arguments he offers there is an account of Kant's text. Thus what I shall do here is state Strawson's theory and, since it is at least analogous to some of Kant's views, go on to ask whether it might be used to interpret Kant.

What, then, is a transcendental argument for Strawson? His general remarks about such an argument are sparse. He says only that such an agument relates to the general structure of our thinking.[15] Let us examine two of the examples he gives of such an argument in order to extract their logical structure. I shall consider the argument against massive reduplication and the argument against skepticism with regard to the numerical reidentification of particulars over periods of interrupted observation. Both of these arguments pertain to our conceptual scheme and both of them are held to be paradigm cases of transcendental arguments.

The argument against massive reduplication runs like this.[16] We are asked to entertain the claim that a particular can be duplicated infinitely. This is a denial of the claim that no particular can be duplicated. To put the same point differently: To say that particulars can be massively reduplicated is to say that no particular has a unique description. But the denial is false because it presupposes the truth of the very claim which it denies; the claim, namely, that every particular is unique. Thus to say that there are particulars which can be duplicated presupposes the existence of one particular answering to the identifying reference of the person making the claim. And this particular is the system of spatiotemporal relations.[17] What guarantees the uniqueness of every particular is this system of relations; and since it is presupposed by the person who asserts that particulars can

15. P. F. Strawson, *Individuals* (London: Methuen, 1959), p. 21.
16. *Ibid.*, pp. 23 ff.
17. *Ibid.*, p. 25.

be duplicated, the proposition asserting uniqueness of particulars is transcendental; or, as Strawson himself puts it, such a proposition states a general feature of our conceptual scheme.

The point of Strawson's argument here can be put as follows. Anyone holding that a particular can be duplicated must assume that there is something with reference to which we can say that a given particular is duplicated as distinct from there being two particulars neither of which is a duplication of the other. This something—the system of spatiotemporal relations—must itself remain numerically identical despite the duplication of things in it. If the system of spatiotemporal relations did not remain numerically identical, then what we call a *duplication* of particulars would really be an exhibition of two different particulars neither of which is a duplication of the other. Thus the possibility of massive reduplication of particulars assumes the existence of a particular that cannot be reduplicated at all.

Consider now the argument against the skeptic's claim that particulars are discontinuous.[18] The skeptic doubts that the particular he sees at one time is numerically the same particular that he sees again once he has interrupted his observation. We are asked to entertain here two different systems of spatiotemporal reference; for only if we can conceive of two such independent systems of reference can we, according to Strawson, doubt that the particular we see at one time is the particular we see at another.

But the skeptic's claim is false because it entails the truth of a proposition which the skeptic wants to deny. Strawson explains this as follows:

> For such a doubt makes sense only if the two systems are not independent, if they are parts, in some way related, of a single system which includes them both. But the condition of having such a system is precisely the condition that there should be satisfiable and commonly satisfied criteria for the identity of at least some items in one sub-system with some items in the other.[19]

The doubt which the skeptic entertains entails the truth of the very proposition which he purports to doubt. For what he doubts is that

18. *Ibid.*, pp. 35 ff.
19. *Ibid.*, p. 35.

there is a unified spatiotemporal framework of reference. But his doubt entails the existence of such a framework. To claim that no particular continues from one observation to another implies that at least the spatiotemporal framework in which the observation takes place continues from one observation to another. Otherwise we could not *say* that the number of particulars we observed was two and not one, for they can be two only with respect to the same framework of identification. And so the proposition that there exists such a framework is basic to our conceptual scheme.

What exactly is the relation between the transcendental proposition and its denial which obtains in these arguments? Take the examples in turn. What is entailed by saying that there are particulars which are not unique? Strawson says that such a claim entails the acceptance of one particular that is unique—the spatiotemporal framework of reference. And it is easy to see that he is right. To say that a particular is duplicated is to say that it is duplicated *in the same framework*, for once it is admitted that there are two frameworks of identification and not one, then it is simply self-contradictory to say that the same particular is in both of them. What makes this so is that the spatiotemporal framework individuates particulars. What makes particulars unique is their location in a single spatiotemporal framework. And to deny that particulars are unique is to assume a framework of identifying them which would make them unique. If it is true to say that there are some particulars that are not unique, then it is true that there is one spatiotemporal framework. And from this it follows that it is false to say that there are particulars which are not unique. The denial of the proposition that particulars are unique entails the truth of its negation.

But what about the proposition that the particular I observe at one time might not be the same particular I observe later? I interpret this claim to mean, not that we can make mistakes about our observation, but rather that *all* the particulars we observe might be discontinuous. What does this proposition imply? Here, again, what is implied is that there is one framework of reference in terms of which we can say that the particulars we observe at one time are not the same as those we observe at another. If there were as many frames of reference as there are particulars, then it would be logically impossible to *doubt* that the particular we observe at one instant is the same particular that we observe at another. For to concede such a plurality of systems of reference is to *know* that the particulars we observe at one time are not the same as those we observe at another. Thus in order to *doubt* the continuity of all particulars, we must assume the continuity of at least one particular. And this entails the falsehood of the claim that no particular is continuous.

The strength of Strawson's argument can, however, be easily misinterpreted. To say that all particulars observed at one time might be different from the particulars one observes at a later time does imply, as Strawson says it does, the acceptance of a single spatiotemporal framework. But this still leaves a modified skepticism open. You can hold, for example, that there is a single spatiotemporal framework and still have doubts about all the particulars within that framework. This kind of skepticism would not fall to the same attack as the kind which extends its claim to cover the frame of reference within which the skeptical doubt is entertained. But once this kind of exaggerated skepticism is advanced, the implication which Strawson thinks is characteristic of a transcendental argument holds: To doubt the continuity of all particulars implies the acceptance of the proposition that one particular is continuous. And thus such a doubt implies its own negation.

Does this theory of transcendental arguments apply to the *Kritik?* There are two reasons why it does not. First of all, the denial of neither the first nor the second Analogy generates its opposite as a deductive consequence. Consider the formulation of these propositions which was given earlier:

1. There are pure intuitions which fall under the concept of the permanent through time.
2. There are pure intuitions which fall under the concept of necessary succession according to a rule.

The contradictories of these propositions are as follows:

1'. No pure intuitions fall under the concept of the permanent through time.

2'. No pure intuitions fall under the concept of necessary succession according to a rule.

Now 1' does not entail 1; nor does 2' entail 2. Thus the denial of a proposition which for Kant is transcendental does not imply its own negation.

There is a second reason why Strawson's theory of transcendental arguments will not do as an exegesis of Kant. If the theory were applied to Kant, it would entail the collapse of Kant's distinction between a dogmatic and a critical proof of a proposition. A dogmatic philosopher seeks to establish truths which are about the world from an analysis of concepts alone. An example of this is the procedure by which the rational psychologist seeks to prove that the ego is a substance: He moves from an analysis of the concept of the ego as subject to the conclusion that it is a substance. To do this is to make a claim about what can be experienced. And the rational psychologist goes wrong when he tries to show that substantial egos *exist* by the analysis of concepts. A critical proof assumes that many of the propositions which are mistakenly taken to be analytically true are really covert existence claims, the truth of which cannot be ascertained by analysis of concepts.

But if Strawson's theory of transcendental arguments is used to explicate Kant, it will entail the consequence that the propositions which Kant thought it possible to prove only critically would have dogmatic proofs. When Strawson shows that a proposition is entailed by its own denial, he draws the inference that it tells us something about our conceptual framework. Thus we cannot deny that particulars lack uniqueness; nor can we deny that all particulars are discontinuous. What should be noticed about these examples of positions which, according to Strawson, are fundamental truths about our conceptual framework is that both are claims about what characteristics an entity can have. They are not existence claims. For this reason, then, we cannot make the immediate inference from the truth of these propositions to the conclusion that they formulate conditions of possible experience. To show that a proposition does state such a condition, it would be necessary to show, not merely that the proposition in question has a self-refuting denial, but that the objects which the propositions are about are conditions of possible experience. And a step which is indispensable to such a demonstration is showing that the objects exist. Strawson's account of transcendental arguments is compatible with the nonexistence of the objects which these arguments concern. To show that a proposition is implied by its own denial is not to show that such a proposition states a categorial feature of the world. Thus Strawson's account leaves out what is most characteristic of the transcendental method as Kant understands it: the distinction between establishing a proposition dogmatically and establishing it critically.

3

The Transcendental Method: Another Account

IS THERE ANY ACCOUNT that can be given of the transcendental method in the first *Kritik* that is free from the defects of the ones which I have so far canvassed? Any such account would have to provide satisfactory answers to three questions: What are the basic propositions from which the method starts? What is the relation between these propositions and those to which we are supposed to argue in the practice of the transcendental method? And, finally, do the propositions which are established by this method have the characteristics of a metaphysical proposition which were set forth at the beginning of this chapter? I shall argue that there is an account which can satisfactorily answer all of these questions.

Consider what is to count as a basic proposition for the method. Such a proposition is neither a description of a commonsensical object nor a description of individual representations. The former is a proposition that admits too much into the proof, while the latter admits too little. What should not be overlooked in the proofs that Kant gives for the Analogies is that he includes the spatial-temporal relations in which representations stand as part of the description from which the method takes its start. Kant does, of course, start with the proposition that all apprehension of the manifold is successive. But he soon supplements that description by pointing out the existence of such relations as irreversibility, in the proof for the second Analogy, and characteristics of time as permanence, in the case of the first Analogy. Thus there is no reason to believe that Kant excludes propositions about relations in which representations stand to one another from counting as basic. What counts as basic, then, is either a proposition which describes a representation or one which describes temporal relations in which those representations stand to one another.

But in what relation do such propositions stand to the propositions which are transcendental? The relation is that of straightforward logical implication. This is less clear in the first than it is in the second Analogy. In the proof for the first Analogy, Kant points out the existence of the relations of coexistence and succession in the manifold.[20] He then concludes that the facts of coexistence and succession in the manifold imply the existence of a permanent element through time so that they can be represented. What we apprehend in the manifold, then, is coexistent and successive representations. But if this is so, then continuants must exist. Otherwise we could not say of representations that are presented successively that they none the less coexist.

A parallel procedure is found in the proof for the second Analogy. There he again points out the successive character of our apprehension of the manifold.[21] But he also shows that there is a temporal relation that is irreversible.[22] This distinction strictly implies, according to Kant, the second Analogy; for if the proposition formulating that Analogy were false, then there would be no irreversible temporal sequences. And so the relation between the basic propositions of the method and transcendental propositions is deductive.

20. B225.
21. A192 = B237.
22. *Ibid.*

This leaves us asking whether the transcendental propositions which are implied by the kind of basic proposition mentioned above really fulfill the requirements of metaphysical propositions. It should be noticed that the transcendental propositions which are implied by both types of basic proposition cannot be analytic: The basic proposition which is the premise of the implication is the claim that certain kinds of relations between representations exist in the manifold. Whatever else they may imply, such claims do imply the existence of whatever is necessary to account for these facts. And this is just that substances and causal sequences exist.

But in what way can such claims as the existence of substances and causes be taken to be universal and necessary? An existence claim that would be universal and necessary in Kant's sense would have the following character: It would be a claim that every object that we experience would instantiate a certain concept. There would, that is, be no experience which would provide us with an object which would fail to instantiate either the concept of substance or that of cause. If the transcendental propositions which are implied by basic propositions have this character, then the account I have given of the transcendental method in the first *Kritik* would fit all of the requirements Kant lays down for that method. But the propositions implied by basic propositions cannot have this character and remain synthetic. The reasons for this will show us the limitations of the method as a way of deciding metaphysical propositions.

4

The Transcendental Method: The Attack Renewed

WHAT, THEN, prevents transcendental propositions from being at once synthetic and universal and necessary? I have already argued that transcendental propositions are existence claims. There are two kinds of objects which fall under the concepts in such propositions. First, there are pure intuitions which correspond to the schematized categories. Secondly, however, there are empirical objects which have categorial characteristics because all empirical objects are subject to pure intuition and its characteristics. If a transcendental proposition is to be universally and necessarily true, all empirical objects would have to fall under the concepts contained in the transcendental proposition. But all empirical objects can do this only if all of them have the characteristics which instantiate schematized categories in pure intuition. And these characteristics do not, as I have argued, serve as adequate instantiations of the concepts of substance and cause. The characteristics which could instantiate such concepts are those which are shared by any manifold whatsoever—even manifolds which are merely successive.

There is one way of repairing this defect. We could distinguish, as Kant himself does, between a broad sense of object as any representation which is present to the mind and a narrow sense in which only spatiotemporal continuants are objects. All of the latter objects do fall under the concepts in transcendental propositions. None of the former does. But this distinction will not help: If objects in the narrow sense must one and all instantiate the categories, transcendental propositions will become universally and necessarily true only by becoming analytic. This can be shown as follows. Suppose that transcendental propositions are construed as existence claims about objects in the narrow sense. This would be a synthetic proposition; but it would not be universal and necessary. For the class of objects in the broad sense is larger than the class of objects in the narrow sense; consequently, there would be some objects about which we would not know whether the categories applied to them or not.

Suppose, however, that transcendental propositions are claims that all objects in the narrow sense must fall under the categories. This would be universally and necessarily true. But it would also be analytic, for what counts as an object in the narrower sense is just what does by definition fall under the categories. The only way in which transcendental propositions can be construed as both synthetic and *a priori*, then, is to show that characteristics of pure intuition instantiate the concepts in such propositions; and from this it would follow that all empirical objects do fall under the schematized categories. Once this way is closed, however, then the only alternative available is to restrict the sense of "object"; and from this it follows that transcendental propositions are either synthetic but *a posteriori* (the domain of representations is larger than the domain of empirical objects) or that they are *a priori* but analytic (all the objects which fall under the concepts in such propositions are defined as objects just because they do fall under those concepts).

This difficulty uncovers both the strength and the weakness of the transcendental method in the first *Kritik*. Both causes and substances are ontological entities. Kant counts as such an entity anything the concept of which belongs to the concept of an object in general. This criterion masks the following ambiguity. To say that substances and causes constitute an object in general is to say, first, that the presence of such entities in experience explains how we can know experiential objects and, secondly, that all of the objects we experience are constituted of substances which stand in causal relation to one another. These claims are very different. You can, for example, argue that such entities as substances and causes exist without having to argue that the propositions asserting their existence are universally and necessarily valid of experience. Thus there are really two issues being raised when Kant asks about the applicability of metaphysical concepts to experience. He is, first of all, asking whether these concepts have referents. He wants to know whether there are any causes and substances. And he is, secondly, asking whether the referents of metaphysical concepts are universal components of every experience. The weakness of the transcendental method is that it gives us no way of proving this second claim. Any such attempt breaks down on the difficulty that a proposition claiming universal and necessary validity for a metaphysical concept would be either analytic or undecidable.

This permits us a better view of the strength of the transcendental method as it is practiced in the first *Kritik*. The method does succeed in prescribing a way of showing how certain problematic entities can be shown to exist. What is problematic about causes and substances is that we are not acquainted with them in the same way that we are acquainted with individual presentations. Consider permanence

through time. What we see in the manifold is a series of presentations. We can bring each of these before our mind; but we cannot
bring the permanent through time before our mind. The same point
can be made for necessary succession according to a rule. We see
events in time; but, however we may be acquainted with causes, we do
not see them as we see the events. Thus neither a substance nor a
cause can be brought before the mind in the way that a single
representation can be brought before the mind.

Yet such entities as substances and causes still exist. And the procedure that Kant follows in part of what he is doing by practicing the
transcendental method is a way of showing this. We see, for example,
that various parts of a stationary object exist at the same time. Even if
we assume that the parts of this single object are not parts of the same
object, we still see that one part exists at the same time as another.
But if this is so, then it follows that something exists through time.
Even though the simultaneously existing parts might belong to different objects, the part we assign to one object must have endured
while we observe the part we assign to another object if we are to say
that the parts are simultaneous. And this implies that there is a
permanent element through time implied by a description we give of
that which we can bring before the mind at one time.

In the same way we can decide whether causes exist. We do note
that we cannot reverse certain sequences of presentations at will. This
implies that we can specify a rule for generating such sequences. And
if this is to be possible, then causes must exist. If they did not, then
there would be no way of specifying rules for generating any kind of
sequence. For the kind of sequence which is given when one event
merely succeeds another cannot be rule-bound. To say that a series is
governed by a rule is to imply that it is possible to break the rule. But
in a series which is determined arbitrarily there can be no violation of
a rule because any order in which the series is generated would count
as an instance of the rule. This is a logical consequence of what we
mean by arbitrary ordering. But since there are sequences which
cannot be arbitrarily ordered, there must be causes.

Both of these arguments illustrate how Kant does prove the existence of substances and causes. But this shows only that more exists than what we can bring before the mind in a single intuitional representation. It does not show that the entities whose existence has been demonstrated in this way are always present in every experience of objects. This can, of course, be shown merely by supplementing the proofs for the existence of entities like causes and substances with the analytic proposition that nothing will count as an object unless such entities are present. But this is less a proof that entities like substances and causes are always present in constituting the objects we experience than it is proof of a determination not to let anything else that might present itself as an object count as such.

INDEX